Modern Tropical

Houses in the Sun | Oscar Riera Ojeda & Byron Hawes

Modern Tropical

Houses in the Sun | Oscar Riera Ojeda & Byron Hawes

RIZZOLI
NEW YORK

New York · Paris · London · Milan

TABLE OF CONTENTS

INTRODUCTION
BY
BYRON
HAWES

"Architecture is the learned game, correct and magnificent, of forms assembled in the light."

—Le Corbusier

Tropical Modern architecture exists within a very specific framework. Myriad inspirations, influences, aesthetics, regional and cultural touchstones coalesce to create a certain something.

More than simply modernist houses based in the tropics, or tropical houses that skew towards modernism, tropical modernism is more than a collocate; rather an imbuement of the essence of modernism into tropical residences, and the soul of the tropics into modern architectural practices.

In exploring Tropical Modern architecture, we must first examine the two halves of the whole. Modern architecture, as it is now known (having been originally introduced to the west predominantly as the International School, through Phillip Johnson's thus-named exhibition at the MoMA in New York), arose

with the Bauhauslers and the Neo-plasticists (the Dutch movement also known as De Stijl) explorations of anti-bourgeoisie, functionality-first design. They were expressed via hallmarks of aesthetic minimalism; including glass corners, flat roofs, honest materials, and expressed structure (as enumerated by Gropius' wife Alma Mahler Gropius Werfel).

And, while modernism was born of the instinct to do away with all that came before; the crenellations, the cornices, the opulence of previous architectural output, it also led naturally into an aesthetic minimalism that lent itself readily to a fluid interaction with its environment; a harmonious subtlety that allowed its environs to shine.

Tropical architecture, on the other hand, has far less specific roots. Initially considered interchangeable with the discipline of vernacular architecture, which specifies design based on local needs, climate, and geography, as well as locally available construction materials, tropical architecture has expanded in definition dramatically, largely based on the output of great architects such as Geoffrey Bawa of Sri Lanka and Luis Barragán of Mexico.

Essentially, tropical modernism is characterized by its adaptation of modern architecture to tropical climes, and to a furtherance of that minimalist aesthetic that has allowed modernism to highlight its environments. Promoting and expanding upon the correlation between built environments and natural ones.

Modern architects believe that 'reading' and 'interpreting' the site of any given project is of crucial importance. That landscape and environment must inspire a project. That a symbiosis between environment and architecture is paramount, and that a structure can and must become a part of its situation. As Charles Eames said, "Recognizing the need is the primary condition for design."

Le Corbusier's "Five Points of a new Architecture" (from his immortal book *Vers Une Architecture*) guided the principles of modernism, but also largely translated directly to inherent principles of tropical architecture. His stipulation of the use of pilotis (reinforced concrete load-bearing columns) in lieu of supporting walls, which offers increased open space, is firmly in line with tropical climates. As was a free design of the ground plan, allowing a more holistic division of spatial usage, rather than traditional splitting of the space into specific rooms. Another of Corbu's points stipulated a roof garden, as a means of bringing nature into the home. While Tropical Modern homes do not implicitly have a roof garden, that integration between indoor and outdoor spaces is a hallmark of the discipline.

These tenets of modernism have proved strongly influential in tropical modernism, though Le Corbusier's vision of a house as "a machine for living" is not strictly adhered to. The great Luis Barragán was an acolyte of Corbusier and the modernists, but, over time, ceased to believe in the functionalist ideology, preferring to strive for an "emotional architecture." This was best expressed in his words "Any work of architecture which does not express serenity is a mistake"; a lucid and straightforward

expression of the essential tenets of tropical architecture. A battle cry for the sublimity of tropical minimalism.

A tropical climate is defined as a non-arid climate in which all twelve months have average temperatures of at least 18° C (64° F). They are frost-free, and weather remains consistently warm year-round.

However, the tropics cannot be easily categorized. Essentially a band traversing the globe between 23.5 degrees north latitude (the Tropic of Cancer) and 23.5 degrees south latitude (the Tropic of Capricorn), the tropical belt encompasses large portions of Central and South America and Africa, parts of North America and Australia, as well as the majority of Africa, Southeast Asia, the South Pacific, and more.

Considering typical modernism's particular adherence to local materiality, climate, culture, and design history, the discipline can range widely in aesthetic and practical terms. Some portions of the tropical belt are arid deserts, others verdant oases of greenery, and still others beachside paradises, prone to prolonged rainy seasons, typhoons, and tropical hurricanes.

Due to climactic disparity, traditional tropical architecture varies widely, from the traditional kampung house of Southeast Asia (raised from the ground on stilts or piles to protect the dwelling from flooding and wildlife) to the modest Adobe houses of the Andes (Adobe naturally functioning as an heat reservoir that stores warmth during the day and metes it out to the dwelling's interior during the cooler evenings due to a time-lag in its absorption of heat through both radiation and convection).

As previously mentioned, tropical architecture can take many forms, depending on, amongst other things, geography. In principle, however, all forms share certain consistent ideals.

Tropical architecture focusses on achieving thermal comfort

through the use of passive design elements including sun-shades, cavity walls, light shelves, overhanging and cantilevered roofs, and shading to block the sun. Open concept floor plans, myriad windows, sliding doors, and louvers allow ingrained ventilation, facilitate air circulation, and control light and shadows.

EXTERNAL INFLUENCES

Strong influencers of tropical modernism can be found in other warm weather (though not strictly tropical) modernist architecture movements.

The Case Study Houses, a programme pioneered by *Arts & Architecture* magazine between 1945 and 1966 specified many of the same intentions, including the need for inexpensive and efficient homes, made from readily available materials. Though, it must be said, materiality for these houses was driven less by locality than by availability of materials post-WWII. Many iconic architects participated in the Case Study programme, including Ray and Charles Eames, Pierre Koenig, Eero Saarinen, and Richard Neutra.

Neutra also played a role in the mid-century modernist movement, a complementary architectural class which also highlighted warm-weather modernist tendencies, largely located in and around the desert area of Palm Springs and the Coachella Valley (typified by Emerson Stewart Williams, William Krisel, John Lautner, Albert Frey, and others). The Sarasota School of Architecture similarly espoused many of the qualities of tropical modernism, based around Western Florida's essentially tropical climate (the area falls just north of the Tropic of Cancer).

LIFESTYLE

"Now I got a house in LA/Now I got a bigger pool than [Kan]Ye."
—Drake

Tropical Modern architecture isn't distinguished simply by aesthetic properties, but often also by the lifestyle it suggests. Yes, it's marked by a rejection of the compartmentalization of in-door and outdoor spaces; and an appreciation of, and interaction with, its surroundings. A direct relationship with nature. Also, if we're honest, a certain feeling of *luxe, calme et volupté*. Tropical Modern architecture has often evoked *La Dolce Vita*. Geoffrey Bawa's iterations of Southeast Asian Long Houses and Balinese courtyards have been reinterpreted into luxurious private residences throughout the region, Vladimir Ossipoff's Shibui-meets-Beaux-Arts piles in Hawaii are emblematic of a specific paradisic dream, and Mario Romañach's pre-Castro Cuban output conjures visions of Errol Flynn and Cary Grant three-martinis-in poolside.

Contemporary Tropical Modern architecture has a version of that stereotype thrust upon it by the uninitiated. Much as Hollywood has often used the clinical geometries and glacial minimalism of mid-century modernists such as John Lautner as a shorthand for baddies (as discussed in DrawDown's 2013 'zine *Evil People in Modernist Homes in Popular Films*), tropical modernism is oft-used as aesthetic short form for a certain lifestyle. Puff Daddy-esque white parties. Billionaire's living large. Max Strang's wondrous RockHouse (page 32) was featured in Michael Mann's major Hollywood film remake of Miami Vice; the Balinese-inspired sanctuary used as the lair of a billionaire South American drug kingpin.

Realistically, real estate in paradise doesn't come cheaply. But as you flip through the pages of this book, I'm sure you'll be struck by the same thought that I am; that, far from suggesting some rock-star lifestyle, each of these houses feels somehow introverted. Private; intimate; quiet. A place of repose, not excess. Oppenheim's spectacularly understated House on as Dune is a whisper, not a holler. It seems to indicate nothing more decadent than a slightly dry, youngish rosé and some lightly grilled local seafood, while the children nap on the chaise as the night's breeze whips softly off the ocean.

MATERIALITY

Materiality is a crucial aspect of vernacular architecture, and a distinct differentialization between the esssential tenets of the disciplines of modernism and tropical modernism.

As you look through this book, you'll see continuous examples of materiality being used to both represent and express local aesthetics and culture. Vo Trong Nghia sourced natural woods and stone indigenous to Vietnam for their Binh House. Juan Puigcorbé built Casa Valle L70 almost exclusively from Melina wood (Gmelina Arborea), a sustainably grown wood so prevalent in local design that it comprises nearly 60 percent of all lumber sourced from forestry plantations in Costa Rica. Chad Oppenheim's House on a Dune uses recycled local cedar, re-used ipe wood, and milk paint, in a nod to the colonial cottages prevalent in its Bahamian environs.

From a materiality perspective, the one constant across all climates and regions tends to be concrete. Inexpensive and efficient, concrete plays strongly into both the aesthetic and political natures of modernism (a more quotidian anti-bourgeois material scarcely exists), while its inherent resilience to inclement weather, low-carbon construction, and geothermal transference properties make it ideal for a wide range of tropical climates.

CONCLUSION

"Simplicity is the ultimate sophistication."
—Leonardo da Vinci

Tropical modernism encompasses myriad styles, cultures, concepts, and materialities; combining them into a cohesive ethos. One that honours nature as it respects and furthers architectural theory. That interprets light and shadow with subtle and lyrical results. That derives great complexity and sophistication through gentle restraint.

For all its complexity, technique, and sociological awareness, it's easy to forget one off the most important things about the houses collected here. They represent some of the best residential architecture from across the globe in recent years. But they are also, quite simply, some of the most beautiful.

35 PROJECTS

Houses in the Sun

Subtropic

TROPIC OF CANCER

Equator

TROPIC OF CAPRICORN

Subtropic

MIA PINE TREE | SAOTA

BRILLHART HOUSE | BRILLHART ARCHITECTURE

ROCKHOUSE | STRANG ARCHITECTURE

4567 PINE TREE DRIVE | STUDIO mk27

1.
MIA PINE TREE
SAOTA

MIAMI, UNITED STATES

House Area:
1,865 m²

Plot Area:
3,575 m²

Architect in Charge:
SAOTA

Project Team:
Philip Olmesdahl, Mark Bullivant
& Andrew Moerdyk

Interior Designer:
Nils Sanderson

Landscape Designer:
Raymond Jungles Inc

Photographer:
Adam Letch

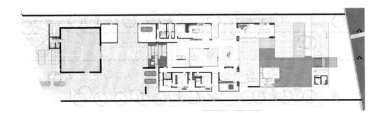

Ground Floor Plan

First Floor Plan

Pine Tree House sees SAOTA's South African design DNA applied to Miami's climate and landscape, retaining their emphasis on the outdoors, and the notion that people live both in and through their homes. In direct contrast to a typical approach of a singular building element on the property, the design is porous, bringing the landscape into the interior of the house. Through the introduction of a collection of introverted and extroverted courtyards, all aspects of the program have an immediate relationship to the outdoors.

The central concept of containment is perhaps best embodied by the screens that cloak the building. Primarily born out of the functional need for privacy and solar control; their application evolved to something far more significant, as CNC punched anodized aluminium became architectural jewellery (as well as nodding in the direction of the intricate brise-soleil of the Californian mid-century modernists). The screens play with the character of light, heightening the experience of enclosure and transparency. In some instances they define spaces (the dou-ble-volume nature of the entrance, for example), in others they result in private, protected sanctuary spaces (bedroom terraces).

While architectural aesthetic is obviously a focus of SAOTA's design team, it is secondary to the functional ways design will be actually be used. This drives how areas are positioned and connected; how the house lives.

This approach extends to the outdoor spaces; a great deal of time and effort went into the design of the rear pool courtyard. In anticipating and elevating the use of outdoor spaces, they were further animated by a series of facilities, including the hot tub, BBQ, bar, and a waterslide. Iconic landscape architect Raymond Jungles imbued the grounds with his relaxed, confident, and freehand approach; resulted in a natural environment that truly reflects Miami.

2.
BRILLHART HOUSE

BRILLHART ARCHITECTURE

MIAMI, UNITED STATES

House Area:
140 m²

Plot Area:
215 m²

Architect in Charge:
Brillhart Architecture

Project Team:
Jacob and Melissa Brillhart

Interior Designer:
Gretel Home

Landscape Designer:
Lin Projects

Photographer:
Bruce Buck, Claudia Uribe Touri, Stefani Fachini

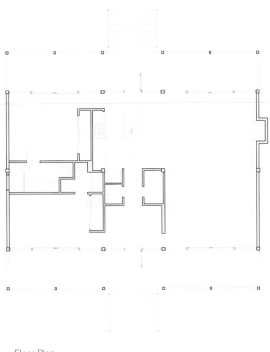

Floor Plan

The 1,500 square foot steel and glass Brillhart house is nestled within the Spring Garden Historic District, one of Miami's oldest neighbourhoods. The architect's goal was to create a new and sustainable architecture for the tropics, beginning with the idea of living in the landscape, centred around questions of minimizing impact on the earth and respect in the context of the neighbourhood.

Some answers came from past building models, particularly the Dog Trot. Historically, the Dog Trot was comprised of two small wooden buildings, connected by a single roof and a central breezeway. The simple structure was both modest and rich in cultural meaning; maximized space and energy, relied on vernacular materials, and celebrated the breeze. The floor plan of the house is a modern interpretation of the Dog Trot, with sleeping quarters on the left and a central corridor (with kitchen) and living space on the right.

Tropical Modern principles—attention to local landscape, marrying building traditions with passive systems, new technologies, and in-

novative construction techniques—also offered direction. Their simple, rational buildings remain models for sustainable design in the tropics. In that spirit Brillhart sought a more sustainable alternative to the use of concrete (the dominant residential building material in Florida), by constructing a steel and glass superstructure.

Floating five feet above the ground, the house is raised as a response to our changing coastal environment. It features four sets of sliding glass doors along the rear elevation, allowing the house to be entirely open. As a result, the landscape functions as the walls of the house. Shutters along the front façade create an outdoor room with shifting shadows, and provide added privacy and protection. These elements allow the house to essentially act as a filter, creating varying levels of transparency.

3.
ROCKHOUSE
STRANG
ARCHITECTURE

MIAMI, UNITED STATES

House Area:
464 m^2

Plot Area:
929 m^2

Architect in Charge:
[STRANG]

Project Team:
Max Strang

Interior Designer:
[STRANG]

Landscape Designer:
[STRANG]

Photographer:
Claudio Manzoni & Claudia Uribe Touri

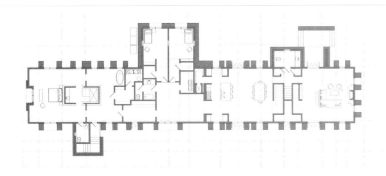

First Floor Plan

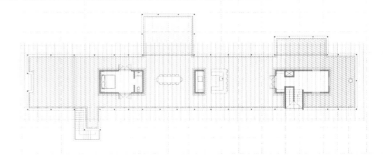

Terrace Floor Plan

In the Southern Miami neighbourhood of Coconut Grove, a veritable subtropical jungle of verdant greenery, lies Strang Architecture's sublime RockHouse. Awash in a sea of Palm Trees, Mangrove, Royal Poincianas, and Strangler Figs, Rock House is a special project, even amongst the collective output of Max Strang's eponymous firm.

Raised in Sarasota, the architectural lessons of Strang's youth heavily influence the majority of his works, with many of the hallmarks of Florida modernism appearing in his designs.

The RockHouse is something special, even for Strang. Heavily influenced by traditional Southeast Asian Longhouse design, Strang built the Rock House for himself and his family. Finding similarities between Coconut Grove's climate and wildlife and that of Southeast Asia, RockHouse is reminiscent of Geoffrey Bawa's Ena de Silva House, with its juxtaposition between the minimalist interior decoration and open floor plans of the Corbusians with iconic elements of South Asian courtyard houses, and his iconic Bentota Beach Hotel, with its overhanging roof and stone walls.

Like Bawa, Strang prioritizes the usage of natural and local materials. He makes great use of oolitic limestone. Stone accents, ipe wood, and polished concrete are used continuously throughout the interior, creating a rich earthy palette of textures and surfaces. A plethora of windows and terrace doors link indoor and outdoor spaces together, creating the sensation of garden spaces less adjacent than interstitial.

Taking further influence from the Case Study Houses of Southern California, particularly Pierre Koenig's Stahl House, RockHouse is delineated into public and private elements, while remaining true to the modernist principles of open-plan layouts. This juxtaposition of flow, organization, and programme creates pockets of private space at the axes, while retaining an overarching open concept.

4.
4567 PINE TREE DRIVE
STUDIO mk27

MIAMI, UNITED STATES

House Area:
1346 m²

Plot Area:
2,200 m²

Architect in Charge:
Studio mk27, Marcio kogan and Lair Reis

Project Team:
Carlos Costa, Constanza Cortes, Diana Radomysler,
Gabriela Chow, Laura Guedes, Mariana Simas,
Raquel Reznicek, Thauan Miquelin

Interior Designer:
Jader Almeida and Artefacto

Landscape Designer:
Raymond Jungles

Photographer:
Fran Parente

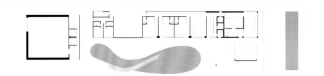

Ground Floor Plan

First Floor Plan

Studio mk27's Pine Tree Drive House is a statement apart, in a town awash with statement architecture; a luxurious Miami Beach residence featuring a private lagoon where residents can swim with fish, and a bridge walkway that snakes over the top.

Measuring 100 feet long (30 metres) and 30 feet wide (nine metres), the manmade lagoon is organically filtered and surrounded by vegetation to provide an "authentically manicured" natural environment. A patio runs alongside the water, featuring a fire pit and benches carved out of tree trunks.

The house is accessed by a wavy 200-foot-long (60 meter) path, which ramps up from the road. Concrete stilts elevate the path above the water, while slats of teak form the balustrade. The two materials also feature prominently throughout the property's interior The walkway provides access to the upper level of the residence, where the main living space is located.

A wall of sliding glass doors open this space up to the terrace, which is bookended by wooden walls and fronted by a glass balustrade. The space overlooks Miami Beach, as well as the rear garden, which features a linear salt-water heated swimming pool.

Part of the floor below is occupied by a generous patio, featuring a sunken lounge area covered by an exposed concrete ceiling. Wooden doors on one side slide open to connect the space with a kitchen, while the doors on the other side reveal windows to the master bedroom suite. This layout allows residents to observe the pool from bed.

A tv room and four bedrooms occupy a second wing, which runs alongside the lagoon. Each room opens onto the patio area.

A green roof tops this volume, while a decked patio is set on the roof of the main house. It is covered with a white canopy and offers a spot for sunbathing.

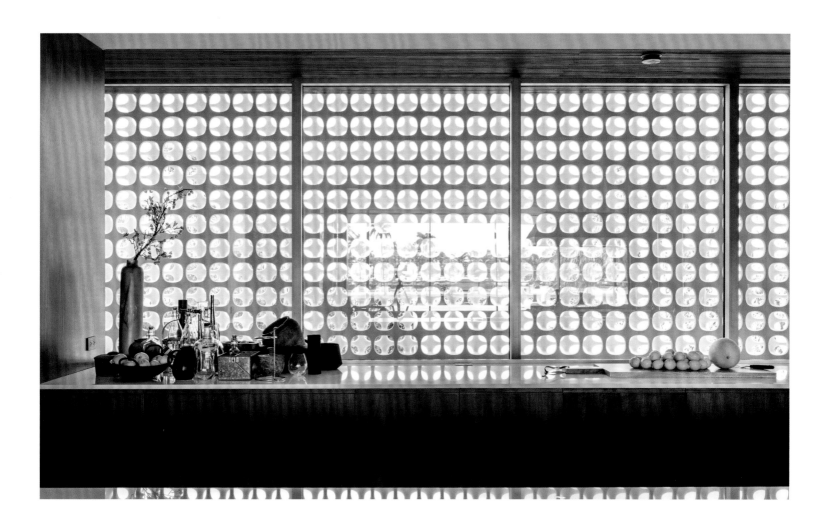

CARIBBEAN & CENTRAL AMERICA

HOUSE ON A DUNE | OPPENHEIM ARCHITECTURE + DESIGN
XIXIM HOUSE | SPECHT HARPMAN
TOUCAN HOUSE | TALLER HÉCTOR BARROSO
LA HOUSE | ELÍAS RIZO ARQUITECTOS
KIMBALL HOUSE | RANGR STUDIO
INOUT HOUSE | JOAN PUIGCORBÉ

5.
HOUSE ON A DUNE OPPENHEIM ARCHITECTURE + DESIGN

BAHAMAS, HARBOUR ISLAND

House Area:
232 m²

Plot Area:
280 m²

Architect in Charge:
Chad Oppenheim

Project Team:
Chad Oppenheim, Juan Calvo, Juan López, Carolina Jaimes,
Jacobus Bruyning, José Ortez, Kevin McMorris, Robert Gallagher,
Francisco Llado, Sebastian Velez, Manuel Morales

Interior Designer:
Oppeneheim Architecture

Landscape Designer:
Oppenheim Architecture

Photographer:
Karen Fuchs

Basement Floor Plan

Ground Floor Plan

Built on a bluff overlooking the swirling cerulean Atlantic waters on the Bahamas' Harbour Island, House on a Dune is built as an open breezeway, providing unfettered views of the dense jungle palms on the inland side, and the ocean on the other. Retractable glass walls offer protection from the elements, while allowing natural light and airflow.

Comprising of a lounge and dining area, the core space is used for meditating, yoga, hosting gatherings, and generally soaking in the picturesque tropical landscape. Living spaces ensconce the central pavilion space, with one side containing two guest suites with ensuite facilities, and the other hosting the kitchen space and master suite.

The house's gabled palm frond roof, made of cedar shakes, simultaneously nods in the direction of the colonial cottages of Bermuda and the Caribbean, and the wide-hewn open-pitched roofs of Southeast Asian vernacular housing. Verandahs extend out from the breezeway, atop a long, meandering staircase of recycled cedar down to the beach, resembling a plinth or viewing platform.

Materiality includes concrete blocks, reused ipe, and milk paint, demonstrably prioritizing locally-sourced materials that imbue the home into its surroundings.

Oppenheim has discussed the influence of the works of conceptualist artist James Turrell on the house's design. Turrell worked often with architectural installations that he called Skyspaces. Specifically proportioned chambers with an aperture in the ceiling open to the sky. Portholes of dimensionality. Ultimately, from a conceptual standpoint, the comparison works, as the experience of standing on this verandah is equivalent to an extra-sensorial experience. Yet, rather than isolating a portion of the view, House on a Dune envisions the entire panoramic view as a skyspace. A view too lush, too luscious, to be compartmentalized.

6.
XIXIM
HOUSE
SPECHT
HARPMAN

TULUM, MEXICO

House Area:
445 m²

Plot Area:
445 m²

Architect in Charge:
Specht Harpman

Project Team:
Scott Specht, Louise Harpman and Brett Wolfe

Interior Designer:
Matthew Finalson

Photographer:
Taggart Sorensen

First Floor Plan

Second Floor Plan

Casa Xixim, located on a narrow site fronting a protected bay in Tulum, Mexico, was designed to be self-sufficient, and to immerse the occupants in the wide range of environments that the site offers.

A path leads from a mangrove marsh, through a palm grove, into a main living space that can be fully opened. The path then continues through a vegetation buffer to the beach beyond. The distinction between interior and exterior dissolves, and house and site merge to become part of one continuous experience. Large full-height and full-width doors allow all rooms to be completely opened to the exterior, creating a perfect harmony between indoor and outdoor spaces. Broad, entirely open-plan communal spaces, delineated only by furniture placement, further enhances the overall sense of freedom and relaxation, as do the myriad outdoor seating areas.

The upper bedrooms of the house open onto a series of crow's-nest terraces, both planted and habitable. The upper roof is a lounge shaded by an overhead solar array. These elevated viewpoints provide another way to experience the surrounding environment, and volumetrically create wildly varying points-of-view and interaction possibilities.

The house is fully self-sufficient, with photovoltaic power generation; on-site waste processing via tank digesters and an artificial wetland; and rainwater collection, storage, and pressurization systems. Passive systems are also used, with louvered doors to capture breezes, and planted roof areas to mitigate stormwater flow.

Materials used in the house were all locally sourced, including louvered wood sliding doors, and hand-painted "pasta tiles." Tulum-based craftsmanship is emphasized, with intricate stonework for selected walls, and site-built furnishings throughout; highlighting many of the aesthetic keystones that have made Tulum a destination for design enthusiasts the world over.

7.
TOUCAN HOUSE
TALLER HÉCTOR BARROSO

VALLE DE BRAVO, MEXICO

House Area:
400 m²

Plot Area:
1,140 m²

Architect in Charge:
Héctor Barroso Riba and Andrea Pérez Salazar

Project Team:
Diego Rentería, Eduardo Carbajal, Vianney Watine

Interior Designer:
Ximena Pérez Salazar

Photographer:
Rafael Gamo

First Floor Plan

Second Floor Plan

Third Floor Plan

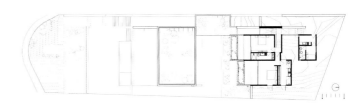

Fourth Floor Plan

Toucan House is located on the top of a hill in Valle de Bravo, on a rectangular plot with a narrow front and a generous extension tapering backwards. The grounds show an upward slope of 46 feet (14 meters) from the entryway to the highest point. Highlighting, rather than working against the uneven topography, the project ultimately developed into a sequence of staggered sections creating pavilions at different levels, which provides the added advantage of maximizing views towards the lake.

The concrete pavilions are demarcated and interrupted by gaps—gardens, terraces, balconies and patios—searching to introduce the interior spaces to the exterior, intentionally making the division between the two almost imperceptible. Reminiscences of the terrain are marked directly into the walls and soil mounds, where the architecture reclines and blends with the site.

Concrete walls and wood ceilings abound throughout the interior spaces, which join the natural ground lower-level sections, which are notably walled on one side by an untreated masonry wall that

runs throughout the house. Largely un-manipulated concrete, stone, steel, and wood constitute the main materials of the house; most of which were sourced locally. Aesthetic decisions based on materiality take into consideration local climate and environment. For example, the concrete walls were made using soil from the site, thereby bringing a light brown color and rougher texture than standard béton brut.

The house merges with the surroundings and becomes part of the natural landscape, allowing contemplation of the surrounding environment. While encompassing and juxtaposing many elements of both traditional local vernacular design and mid-century tropical modernism, this house clearly respects its environment. Nature—the wind, natural light and sounds—take possession and become central components of the house. As they should.

8.
LA HOUSE
ELÍAS RIZO
ARQUITECTOS

MEXICO

House Area:
866 m²

Plot Area:
933 m²

Architect in Charge:
Elías Rizo Suárez and Alejandro Rizo Suárez

Project Team:
Paola Herández and Jenny Mora

Interior Designer:
Kárima Dipp

Photographer:
Marcos García

First Floor Plan

Second Floor Plan

A stark, angular exploration of environment and ethos; Rizo's LA House is a spatial marvel of palettes and open-air exploitations.

The main entry into the complex proceeds to an open passageway that runs along a rough-hewn stone wall and postpones access to the house while creating a feeling; an essence. A glazed box containing a studio protrudes from the building; hovering above a large pond that can be crossed via a series of stone pavers that rise above the water and lead directly into the house's public areas. The garage, concealed beyond the stone wall, compels cars to park sideways so as to render them invisible from all spaces in the house.

The entry sequence into the building presents as a series of layers, starting with the garden space beyond the setback lines, following through the open corridor past the pond, and crossing through the central courtyard all the way to the living spaces at the back of the main pavilion.

A central courtyard scheme was implemented to introduce natural ventilation into every space of the house without compromising privacy. The corridors around the courtyard on the ground floor are defined by a series of operable windows that allow the kitchen and living spaces to bleed out into the exterior, when the weather allows it. Similarly, a small, glazed atrium ventilates the master bathroom, and deeply recessed balconies yield generous exterior areas to all bedrooms.

Crossing the lawn, beyond the living spaces on the ground floor, a pool and a concrete volume containing an entertainment room overlook a small ravine. Below this volume a staggered pathway descends gently to negotiate the changes in topography on a pronounced cliff.

Dark gray steel, glass, wood, concrete, and stone compose the greater part of the material palette throughout the house, which is complemented by accents in leather and stainless steel.

9.
KIMBALL
HOUSE
RANGR
STUDIO

NAGUA, DOMINICAN REPUBLIC

House Area:
173 m²

Plot Area:
8,093 m²

Architect in Charge:
Rangr Studio

Project Team:
Jasmit Singh Rangr, Eivind Karlsen and Josh Weiselberg

Interior Designer:
Monica Bouwmeester and Rangr Studio

Landscape Designer:
Monica Bouwmeester and Rangr Studio

Photographer:
Hilary Ferris White

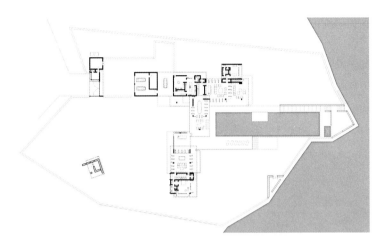

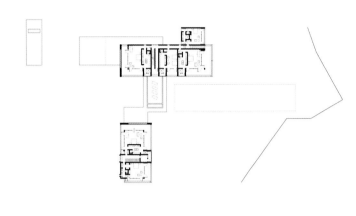

Ground Floor Plan

First Floor Plan

Situated on a cliff on the north coast of the Dominican Republic, with a panoramic view of the Atlantic Ocean, each of eight Casa Kimball's suites has a breathtaking view out to the ocean.

Throughout the property, interior spaces merge with exterior spaces, all of which are designed to allow ocean breezes under shade from the sun. Light at sunset rakes through trees, casting dappled sunlight on the light stone floors in the evening.

Case Kimball is comprised of two buildings arranged in L formation. A low connecting piece between the two contains the entranceway, dining room, and an outdoor lounge and bar. The connector floats above the ground forming a plinth, centred on a view of the pool and ocean beyond. The two main buildings are conceived of as floating rectangles that have come to rest on volumes that engage the ground. These ground volumes are covered in split-face Coralina, while the rectangular cuboids are covered in smooth Coralina, heightening the effect of "floating volumes" versus "ground volumes." All of the gi-

gantic window-door panels open at the public levels, creating seamless flow from inside to outside, from gardens to pool.

The 148-foot-long (45 meter) salt pool forms the centerpiece of Casa Kimball. Every room in the house has a view of the infinity edge and ocean beyond. Three different levels of platforms within the pool allow guests to lie flat in the water, sit, and lounge. Using a deep blue slightly reflective tile, the pool's surface changes color to match the ocean—gray, aquamarine, and deep blue. As the sun sets behind the house, the sky above the ocean turns a deep blue and is reflected in the pool's water. It creates a rational rectangle of water against the turbulent ocean. Swimming in the pool out toward the ocean creates the illusion of being in the ocean itself, one sees nothing but the endless horizon where water meets sky.

10.
INOUT
HOUSE
JOAN
PUIGCORBÉ

SAN JOSE, COSTA RICA

House Area:
651 m²

Plot Area:
1,320 m²

Architect in Charge:
Joan Puigcorbé

Project Team:
Carolina Pizarro

Interior Designer:
MKBstudio

Landscape Designer:
Maria K Hawkins

Photographer:
Jordi Miralles

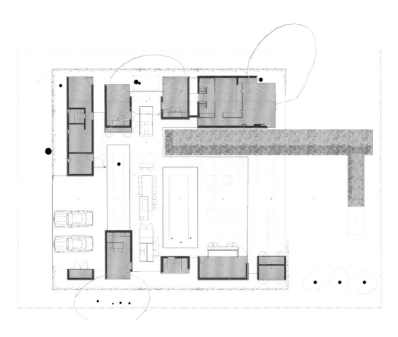

First Floor Plan

Joan Puigcorbé's InOut House is named for its uninterrupted 'inside-outside' relationship; a sequence of layers between the open and the intermediary. Frontal boundaries are blurred by sheets of glass and vegetation, framed by two horizontal planes, floor and ceiling, where the full and the void are related via a series of matter, water, vegetation, and the sky. Lateral boundaries establish the "full-void" relationship via a series of solid materials that close transversal views.

All bedrooms are arranged along the peripheries bordering the neighbors, leaving an intermediate space between volumes for social uses; kitchen-dining, living room, swimming pool, porch and barbecue.

A perimeter curtain of rope and vegetation delineates the limits of the building element, creating a gap of shadow and light that qualifies a space between. A single material, melina wood, dresses the inside and the outside. The apparatus varies: the outside is expressed as a relief while the inside is softened.

In a further collocation of the in-and-outdoors, existing trees remain in the spaces that they did pre-build, uncompromisingly piercing various spaces of the house. The kitchen and kitchen table shape a sculptural floor that presides over the social zone. The black gloss of the absolute black granite dematerializes, through its reflections, the gesture of formal forcefulness.

This house responds to the existing features of the landscape and reveals new dimensions of the topography of place. In its formalization and materiality, the experience of light, shadow, earth, water and air is intensified. The general form is readily readable, and fluid in its articulation of space, while a t-shaped reflecting pool juts out from the main living spaces, further bringing the sky and moon directly inside the structure.

SOUTH AMERICA

11.
TWO BEAMS
HOUSE
YURI VITAL

TIBAU DO SUL, BRAZIL

House Area:
107 m²

Plot Area:
220 m²

Architect in Charge:
Yuri Vital

Project Team:
Bruno Santucci, José Amorim and Roni Ebina

Interior Designer:
S + N Architecture and Interiors

Landscape Designer:
Yuri Vital

Photographer:
Nelson Kon

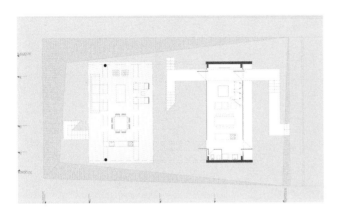

Ground Floor Plan

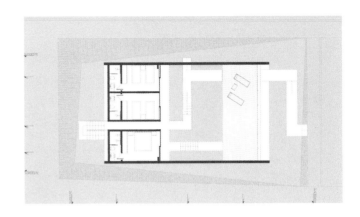

First Floor Plan

One of the central themes of modernism is paring things down to their essence. Mies said "less is more," Rams said "as little design as possible." Yuri Vital holds those tenets up in his brilliant Two Beams House.

Essentially a concrete frame, the house is supported only by two beams and four pillars, made entirely of concrete, in a sort of pared-down Tadao Ando-esque minimalist masterpiece. Vital set out to create a home with an entirely new concept; breaking paradigms and pushing the boundaries. He based the house on three fundamental aims; view, ventiliation, and natural lighting.

The one floor residence is disposed in two pavilions, with five feet (1.5 meters) in height between them, connected by a set of stairs, and allowing ocean and garden views from all space. A void at the bottom, which is formed due to the difference of levels, works as a communal space for recreation, gatherings, or repose. Over the front pavilion and through the stairs there is a solarium, where the sea view is highlighted, as the viewer is above tree level unfettered

views are provided. A small canopy of trees along the sun-facing elevation generate shade in the lower pavilion; utilizing nature to assist in creating a comfortable climatic nature indoors.

Materiality is locally sourced and highly environmentally conscious. Concrete, glass, treated wood, and anticorrosive metals combine to compound the spatiality and volume of the house, in a fit of modern minimalism.

House as viewing box. Simple, inexpensive, endlessly reproducible. Truly an exemplar for a new residential typology.

12.
GAF HOUSE
JACOBSEN
ARQUITETURA

SÃO PAULO, BRAZIL

House Area:
1,398 m²

Plot Area:
1,660 m²

Architect in Charge:
Paulo Jacobsen and Bernardo Jacobsen

Project Team:
Edgar Murata, Marcelo Vessoni, Jaime Cunha Jr., Christian Rojas,
Henrique Vetro, Maya Leal

Interior Designer:
Jacobsen Arquitetura

Landscape Designer:
Bonsai Paisagismo

Photographer:
Fernando Guerra | FG+SG

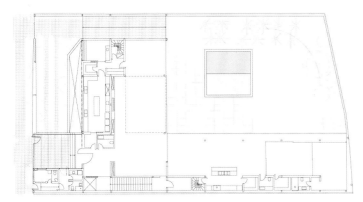

Ground Floor Plan

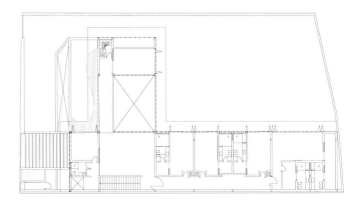

First Floor Plan

A wide, low slung, modernist masterpiece, the GAF House is a symphony of architectural simplicity. With an upper floor entirely enveloped by a wooden skin consisting of mobile and fixed panels, structured in metallic frames, it provokes the sensation of being entirely encompassed in brise soleil.

The development of this element, which was entirely custom, required special opening systems. In addition to providing visual protection and a unique identity for the project's façade, the wood panels allow for extensive natural light and ventilation, and create a dimension through the interplay of light and shadow, causing geometric shadows to dance across the walls; almost a natural in situ art installation rippling with the afternoon sun.

The L-shaped project was built within the frontal boundaries and one of the sides of the ground floor. Thus, in addition to creating physical and visual protection against the street, releasing a maximum amount of space for the garden, with complete pri-

vacy yet greater sunlight. The square shape of the pool formally represents and highlights the importance of this open, communal area, which functions as the spatial core of the house and all of the residents' activities.

The programme of the house is based on clear compartmentalization; with the garage and service area underground; the living, dining, kitchen and verandas on the ground floor; and the bedrooms, family room and office on the upper floor, creating a clear delineation between public and private spaces.

The main floor is entirely open to the garden and swimming pool; with nearly all spaces highlighted by a transparent interplay with the landscape; combining indoor and outdoor spaces into a cohesive environment. The garden itself, featuring landscaping by Bonsai Paisagismo, continues the geometric cohesion by way of alternating square concrete steps across the grass.

13.
JUNGLE HOUSE
STUDIO mk27

GUARUJÁ, BRAZIL

House Area:
805 m²

Plot Area:
1,668 m²

Architects in Charge:
Marcio Kogan and Samanta Cafardo

Project Team:
Carlos Costa, Eline Ostyn, Laura Guedes, Mariana Ruzante,
Mariana Simas, Oswaldo Pessano, Fernanda Neiva

Interior Designer:
Diana Radomysler

Landscape Designer:
Isabel Duprat

Photographer:
Fernando Guerra | FG+SG

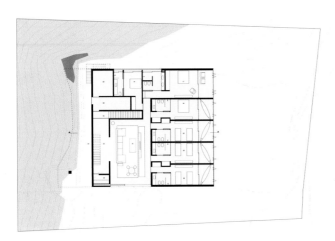

First Floor Plan

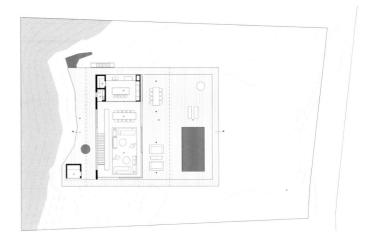

Second Floor Plan

Located on the paulista shore, surrounded by rain forest and a densely vegetative mountainous topography, the Jungle House is marked by a connection between architecture and nature, privileging the view looking out to the ocean and the incidence of sunlight in its internal spaces.

The main volume of the house is elevated from the ground and seems built into the topography. The house, therefore, projects itself out from the mountain. Contact elements between the slope and the construction—for example the wooden decks— were shaped to respect the existing land, thereby creating an organic interaction between nature and the architectural elements.

The 3 floors of Jungle House create a clear programmatic division: the ground floor houses a large covered wooden deck, connected to a small room for the children; on the first floor there are six bedrooms—five of them with small verandas with hammocks —and a tv room; the third and last floor is the social area of the house, including a swimming pool, a living room and the kitchen.

The landscape recomposes the native species. When one is in the house, the relationship with the surrounding vegetation occurs not only through the view but also through the plants that surround the wooden decks. On the ground floor, you can stroll in the midst of trees; on the first floor, light enters filtered through the tree-tops; and on the roof, the house is framed by vegetation, and filtered through an ocean view.

The architecture of the house privileges the use of exposed concrete and wood, as much in both interior and exterior spaces. The bedrooms have wooden sun-screens mounted as folding doors that can be manipulated by users according to climactic needs.

14.
WHITE HOUSE
STUDIO mk27

SÃO SEBASTIÃO, BRAZIL

House Area:
492 m²

Plot Area:
590 m²

Architect in Charge:
Marcio Kogan and Eduardo Chalabi

Project Team:
Eline Ostyn, Maria Julia Herklotz, Laura Guedes, Mariana Ruzante,
Mariana Simas, Oswaldo Pessano, Ricardo Ariza

Interior Designer:
Diana Radomysler

Landscape Designer:
Passe_Ar Verde Paisagismo

Photographer:
Fernando Guerra | FG+SG

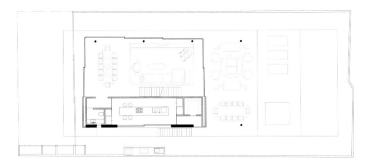

Ground Floor Plan

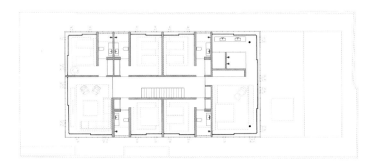

First Floor Plan

A collaboration between mk27's primary architect, Marcio Kogan, and Eduardo Chalabi, the White House is a Corbusian homage par excellence, nestled on a lovely Brazilian beach, on the northern coast beyond São Paolo. Programme and materiality takes into careful consideration both residents' comfort, and upkeep of the building, with regards to the high temperatures and sea air of the local climate.

All of the ambients have floor-to-ceiling window frames—in the spans, like true walls of sliding glass—thereby creating a pleasant thermal sensation and blurring the division between interior and exterior spaces. In the living room on the ground floor, for example, glass doors are built into the walls and integrate the indoor space with the balcony. This creates cross ventilation with the aim of reducing room temperature. In the same space, wooden perforated doors—like large muxarabis—shade the interior without blocking the breeze.

The ground floor contains the entire social area of the house, including the kitchen, which faces one of the side gardens. The first floor, in turn, houses the bedrooms, while there is a terrace garden and deck on the roof—accessible by a flight of stairs protected by a hatch door.

Warm materials are meshed into the metal brises, shading the room on the upper volume. The combination of wood, concrete, and white aluminum (which was chosen for its resistance to the effects of the sea air) are perfectly in keeping with the nature of tropical minimalism.

The large upper volume, cantilevering over the open terrace, rests on a pair of pilotis, in a nod to Corbusian International Style architecture, while the usage of large-scale reflecting pools integrates the landscaping and highlights the Brazilian modernist nature of the space.

15.
HOUSE IN
UBATUBA
SPBR
ARQUITETOS

UBATUBA, BRAZIL

House Area:
346 m²

Plot Area:
887 m²

Architect in Charge:
Angelo Bucci

Project Team:
Ciro Miguel, Juliana Braga, João Paulo Meirelles de Faria,
Flávia Parodi Costa, Tatiana Ozzetti, Lucas Nobre, Nilton Suenaga

Interior Designer:
Ricardo Heder

Landscape Designer:
Raul Pereira

Photographer:
Nelson Kon

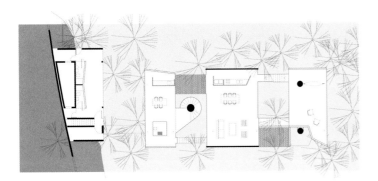

First Floor Plan

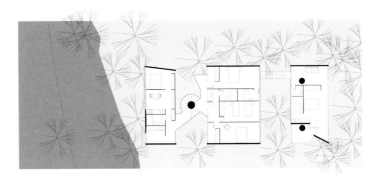

Second Floor Plan

Ubatuba is one of the most important coastal cities in the state of São Paulo, Brazil. It is placed exactly on the Tropic of Capricorn and is very well known as one of the most raining area in Brazil. The House in Ubatuba, which is located on a 180-foot-by-62-foot (55-meter-by-16-meter) ground plot, at the far right end of Tenório Beach, borders on the seashore at one side and goes up a 50 percent slope hill, only reaching street level at 92 feet (28 meters).

The goal of preserving the trees that cover the hill, and that topography as much as possible, inspired the entire strategy used in the conception of the project: not touching the ground unless absolutely necessary. Three columns, of reinforced concrete, support the house. They correspond to the only points where the house touches the ground.

The programme of the house is inverted from bottom to top, with the rooftop terrace being at street level. A bridge connects the street to the main entrance of the house, allowing different views through the trees to both the sea and hills beyond. The swimming pool was placed at this level, in order to absorb maximum sunlight. The pool reflects the surrounding landscape, but also acts as a natural strategy for thermal insulation, while also preventing membrane and other elements on the slab.

The house was conceived as a full-time residence for the commissioning couple, as well as a vacation house for their son and daughter. Therefore, bedrooms were displayed in two completely distinct blocks. The master bedroom, which is placed on the extreme east —facing closer to the sea—is protected by a movable wood louver. The larger group of three bedrooms, is placed behind this first one, while vertically displaced five feet (1.5 meters) below the bottom of the first in order to allow unfettered views to the beach.

16.
OS HOUSE
JACOBSEN
ARQUITETURA

BRAGANÇA PAULISTA, BRAZIL

House Area:
1,200 m²

Plot Area:
3,670 m²

Architect in Charge:
Paulo Jacobsen and Bernardo Jacobsen

Project Team:
Paulo Jacobsen, Bernardo Jacobsen, Edgar Murata, Marcelo Vessoni, Francisco Rugeroni, Luiz Martinelli, Tatiana Kamogawa, Thauan Miquelin, Maya Leal, Mariana Ferretti

Interior Designer:
Marina Linhares

Landscape Designer:
Isabel Duprat

Photographer:
Fernando Guerra | FG+SG

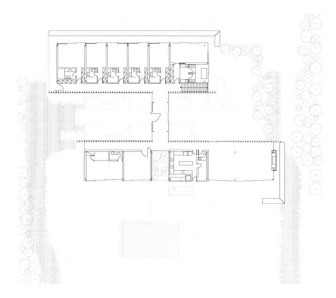

Ground Floor Plan

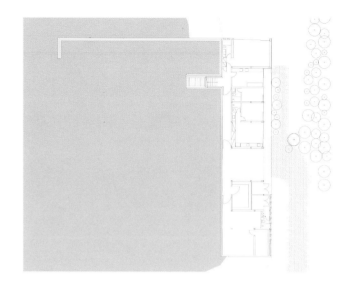

Underground Floor Plan

A symphony of soft light and soft wood; Jacobsen Arquitectura's OS House takes cues from Brazilian modernism (notes of Robert Burle Marx and Rino Levi abound) and post-Corbusian International-Style modernism equally.

Interspersing landscape and traditional architecture into a cohesive aesthetic whole, the most elevated part of the outwardly sloping property was chosen for the house's footprint, allowing greater visual amplitude and lower interference from neighbouring constructions; freely exposing the architecture, the garden, and the swimming pool.

Social and private areas of the house are divided into two parallel cores with the same width; each being disposed and unaligned. The areas are connected through a circulation area on top of a water mirror/reflecting pool, which also functions as the entry hall.

The central communal spaces open up onto a continuous terrace, which provides sprawling views, while a louvred wooden overhang provides protection from the afternoon sun. The pool and solarium are also directly connected to the terrace, and act as a visual obstacle between the house and the street.

The second core is located on the backside of the allotment, and is occupied by family and visitor suites. These accommodations provide opportune views of sunrise and sunset, and have a generous covered terrace, which also acts as an eave to the openings.

The structure is composed of a laminated wood, which echoes the firm's earlier JN house, presenting a succession of slatted porticos; nodding in the direction of the brises-soleil of the Sarasota School.

17.
LLM HOUSE
OBRA
ARQUITETOS

SÃO JOSÉ DOS CAMPOS, BRAZIL

House Area:
1,185 m²

Plot Area:
3,600 m²

Architect in Charge:
João Paulo Daolio, Thiago Natal Duarte

Project Team:
Diogo Cavallari

Landscape Designer:
Panorama Pasagismo, Catê Poli Paisagismo

Photographer:
Nelson Kon

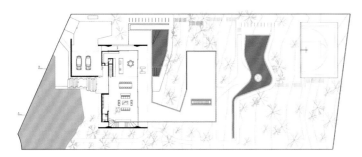

Ground Floor Plan

First Floor Plan

A symphony of metal and glass, nodding gently in the aesthetic direction of the Eames House in the Palisades and the lush indoor/outdoor landscape environs of Sergio Bernardes' Hotel Tambaú, Obra's LLM House is a worthy addition to the Brazilian modernist canon.

Situated on a site already blessed with a plethora of protected native trees, and an average slope of 30 percent, the firm implemented the project as an intensely aware dialogue with the existing topography and vegetation.

With a client mandated build area and programme in the vicinity of 1,200 square meters the architects nonetheless endeavoured to create a space where residents could have direct eye contact and interaction, despite being in different environments/levels of the house. Since this is a single-family residence, it was felt that this approach allows a sense of family, community, and closeness, despite the sheer size of the space.

The greater programme was arranged so that collective spaces; living, working, cooking, and so on, have a direct relationship with landscape views, and higher light intensity. The bedrooms and other private areas are positioned below the treeline, forming a courtyard of tree trunks.

The house was designed in mixed materiality and structure. Retaining walls are done in reinforced concrete, and two gables also specifically serve for adjustment of some quotas of the land and anchoring to the metal frame, hoisted on the trees. This also provides both a delicately industrial, modernist sense, but also further reinforces the interaction between architecture and nature.

AFRICA

QUEROL HOUSE | ALBERTO MORELL
DALTON HOUSE | ALBERTO MORELL

18.
QUEROL
HOUSE
ALBERTO
MORELL

KAREN, NAIROBI, KENYA

House area:
400 m²

Plot area:
1,430 m²

Architect in Charge:
Alberto Morell

Project Team:
David Querol, Elena Velilla, Cobean Designs Nairobi,
Ariadna Barrio, Alba Balmaseda,Tomás Muñoz

Interior Designer:
Alberto Morell

Landscape Designer:
Alberto Morell

Photographer:
Javier Callejas

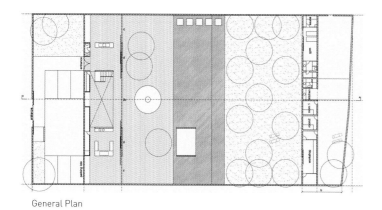

General Plan

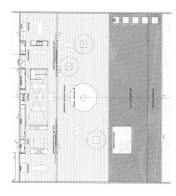

Ground Floor Plan

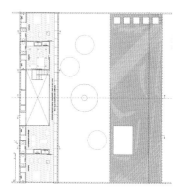

First Floor Plan

Situated in Kenya's capital region of Nairobi, Alberto Morrell Sixto's stunning Querol House is intuitively camouflaged by its own façade. Manifesting as a large-scale, bunker-like concrete box from the exterior; it opens up into a modular framework that references its own concrete form work, via a series of sliding wooden doors. With this house, Alberto Morrell sought to qualify privacy and openness as a pivotal theory within the space, as a character of spatial integration.

The entire house is a single form building; a signature trait of the architect, who is famous for simplifying the idea of space. The 'box' itself divides the site into graduated sectors; a main public area and a vast back yard that opens up into a pool area and an unfettered horizon experience.

The highly contemporary concept—a distinct nationality of self-contained, single structure, highly compartmentalized private residential architecture—is made all the more notable through the robust integration of the building within the site in sub Saharan Africa.

The house boasts a cohesive materiality; the stark contrast of the concrete, the white washed walls and timber carefully and almost seamlessly forming elements of the building that ultimately encompass the building's feeling and weather barrier.

The austere and minimalist façade—only broken by functional windows at the front and sliding doors that open up the house and transform its shape—almost entirely sees an adroit way of dealing with the static and dynamic character of architecture and exposes the building to alternative looks and feel at any given time.

Oscillating between complete openness between all spaces, and utter privacy, Morrell's minimalist typology has been ably articulated, in a thoroughly original and adaptable spatial dynamic.
.

19.
DALTON
HOUSE
ALBERTO
MORELL

MADETENI, KILIFI, KENYA

House Area:
342 m²

Plot Area:
30,000 m²

Architect in Charge:
Alberto Morell

Project Team:
Helen Dalton, Douglas Lackey, Nigel Watson,
Anderson Ngumbao, Nigel Watson, Danji Naran,
Alberto Morel, Raúl Gantes, Tomás Muñoz,
Jorge Reinlein, José María Ordovás

Interior Designer:
Alberto Morell

Landscape Designer:
Alberto Morell

Photographer:
Javier Callejas Sevilla

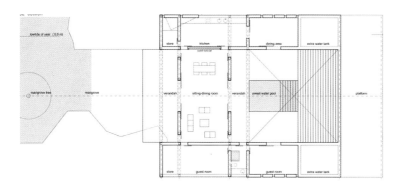

Ground Floor Plan

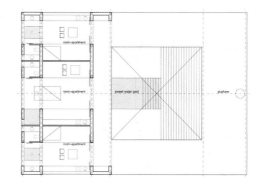

First Floor Plan

Nestled on three acres of the Kenyan beach area of Kilifi, on the Indian Ocean, the Dalton House is situated between the sea entrance in the coral cliff and the back of the mangrove that dots the area. As such, the house's design seamlessly leads into its surrounding environs; the Indian Ocean on the upper floor, and the mangrove on the ground floor. This position between the entrance of the sea and the land's vegetation ensures natural ventilation.

The sea entrance in the cliff determines the width of the house's courtyard and staircase, which has a small swimming pool, and connects the ground and upper floors. These stairs are the sole interaction between the two stories; giving the house the feeling of having two distinct properties in one; the courtyard house downstairs and the platform house above.

Common areas are entirely on the ground floor; including living room, dining room, kitchen, and guest rooms. The top floor contains three small apartments, with a small kitchen and bathroom in each.

The house is built from inexpensive and accessible local materials. The structure—columns and slabs—are concrete, and the space in-between the structure is filled with small coral stones acquired in a local quarry. The floors, walls, stairs, shells, etc. are finished in a local stucco called Lamu; which is easily cared for, clean, soft, and resistant.

All carpentry, doors and windows are made of mahogany. They are carved in homage to a geometric pattern of the mosaics in the Alhambra Palace of Granada, Spain; which has been influential in many Muslim buildings of this Swahili area in Kenya.

Interior spaces are delineated by screens or diaphragms; establishing a continuous and compartmentalized space. This type of space is typical of the ancient Swahili architecture of the Kenyan coast, as well as much traditional Muslim architecture worldwide.

SOUTHEAST ASIA

20.
DIYA
SPASM
DESIGN
ARCHITECTS

AHMEDABAD, INDIA

House Area:
1,432 m²

Plot Area:
10,929 m²

Architect in Charge:
Divyesh Kargathra

Project Team:
Sangeeta Merchant, Divyesh Kargathra, Gauri Satam,
Mansoor Ali Kudalkar, Sanjeev Panjabi

Interior Designer:
SPASM Design Architects

Landscape Designer:
Gsa (Green Space Alliance)

Photographer:
Photographix – Sebastian & Ira, Divyesh Kargathra

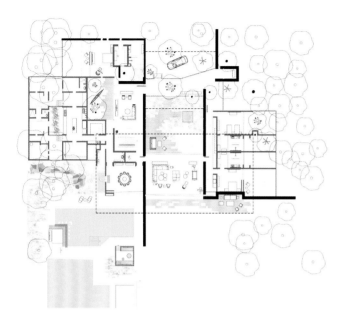

Ground Floor Plan

First Floor Plan

In designing Diya, which translates into "the light that enlightens," and is also the name of the client's daughter, Spasm had to be aware of specific climatic concerns. Ahmedabad is predominantly dry throughout the year, but monsoon season sees major rain.

Tropical modernism has always espoused a certain oneness with nature; a melding of the in-and-outdoors; but Diya doubles down on that conceit by not only ensconcing the residence in lush greenery, but building trees directly into certain transitory spaces. Poetically, the trees seamlessly intersperse into the ceiling and floor, never really beginning or ending. As much Joyce as Olmsted.

284 trees existed on the property prior to the build, and each was retained. Foundations were hand dug to preserve roots, with the trees ultimately functioning as generators of specific vistas and open-air courtyards, resulting in a formless labyrinth of interconnected spaces.

The entryway is marked by a 52 foot (16 meter) columned, free span canopy, which creates an 8 foot (2.4 meter) high entry space bound by vertical pivoting wooden louvers. Functioning like a filter, the entryway allows breezes to freely flow through to the main courtyard beyond, and frames a pre-existing neem tree as sculpture, announcing the house's environmental ambitions from the onset.

The house's ground level, bound by massive rammed earth walls, multiple courtyards, vertical pivoting wooden louvers, and sliding glass walls (which retract into pockets) allows the living and dining spaces to seamlessly connect with verdant outdoor areas.

The upper storey is sheathed in corten, with 18-by-1.5-foot (5.5 by 0.5 meter) panels which hang off the internal structure, crating a ventilated façade, which absorbs heat and allows air circulation. The corners of the volume are perforated as Jaalis, in patterns of trees and branches, a nod to the Sidi Saiyyed Mosque Jaali, an architectural wonder of Ahmedabad.

21.
RETREAT
IN THE
SAHYADRIS
KHOSLA
ASSOCIATES

WESTERN GHATS, MAHARASHTRA,
INDIA

Area:
195 m²

Plot:
8,093 m²

Architect in Charge:
Sandeep Khosla and Amaresh Anand

Project Team:
Sandeep Khosla, Amaresh Anand, Oommen Thomas,
Pratyusha Suryakanth and Moiz Faizulla

Interior Designer:
Khosla Associates

Landscape Designer:
Transcapes

Photographer:
Shamanth Patil J.

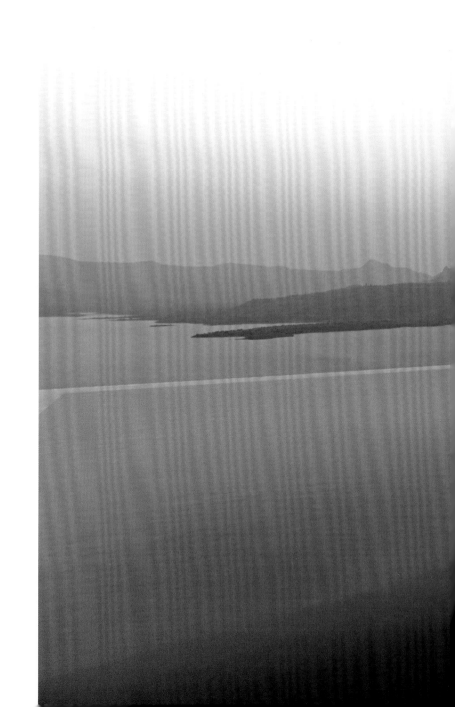

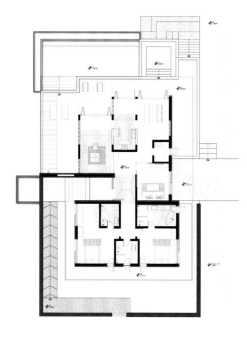

Ground Floor Plan

Khosla's residence was conceived as a single-story pavilion pied-à-terre. The client's primary mandate was engaging with the site's natural surroundings, including a panoramic view of the lake and the imposing mountain ranges beyond.

Spatially subdivided into two primary zones; one for engagement with the view during the day, and the other as a place for night-time retreat and repose. The public zone to the west houses the living, dining, and open-concept kitchen that opens out into a large deck with sunken seating, infinity pool, and the expansive views. The private zone to the east houses two bedrooms, and opens into an intimate sunken courtyard. One side is extroverted and permeable, allowing nature to penetrate its envelope; the other is introverted and protected.

A central instinct of the house's design was to utilize and modulate natural light both in external spaces and throughout the internal volumes. To this end, a series of dramatic skylights were installed, in order to illuminate internal spaces evenly. The angular shape of the skylights were inspired by the looming profiles of the neighbouring mountain peaks.

The house is built primarily from readily available local black basalt stone, which was sourced on-site, using it as a dry pack cladding, as well as on internal accent walls. The remainder of the shell is natural and monochromatic; using polished cement plaster, while flooring is done in slabs of river-finished and polished brown Kota stone. Window boxes are crafted of sustainable Accoya wood, and open to the deck and swimming pool via sliding and folding vertical panels.

The overall intent of the retreat is encapsulated in a few bold gestures; a box sitting on a plinth, a hovering roof form protecting it from sun and rain, and random apertures admitting soft light within.

22.
THE TWIN HOUSES SPASM DESIGN ARCHITECTS

ALIBAG, INDIA

House Area:
1,142 m²

Plot Area:
8,100 m²

Architect in Charge:
SPASM Design Architects

Project Team:
Sangeeta Merchant, Mansoor Kudalkar, Vijjisha Kakka,
Noopur Sejpal, Divyesh Kargathra, Sanjeev Panjabi

Interior Designer:
SPASM Design Architects

Landscape Designer:
Kunal Maniar and Associates

Photographer:
Photographix – Sebastian & Ira

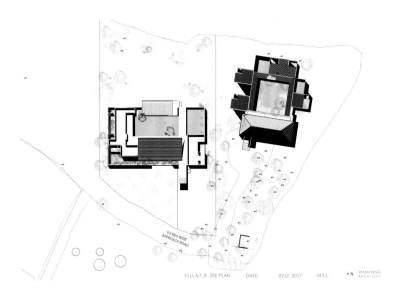

Villa 7 and 8, Site Plan

A pair of complementary courtyard homes; the Twin Houses comprise of a single, fully ground-hugging single-level structure, with the other echoing that typology, but adding a pavilion-esque living room and pool on the upper level.

The two halves of the site share a common boundary, but have very different characteristics. One was a flatland overlooking pastoral hills to the west; the other dotted with mango trees.

Construction materials are simple and refined, utilizing unfinished béton brut concrete, various local timbers, and black industrial aluminium for supporting beams and window frames. Open concept courtyards, Bauhaus style supporting pilotis, and wide overhanging roofs nod to the central tenets of the genre.

Villa 7 is enclosed within a 10 foot (3 meter) high red laterite wall crafted in the manner of a temple plinth, which has a 40 foot (12 meter) wide central opening onto the views of the hills and lawn beyond. The opening straddles a swimming pool, forming

a foreground to the verdant view beyond. The entire courtyard is edged with a 10 foot (3 meter) wide verandah, allowing for protected movement between rooms. As such, the pool, which is a focal point, becomes a transitory threshold between the house, the contained courtyard, and the grounds beyond.

Villa 8 exists on a smaller scale, but echoes its larger brother. The verandah is 5 feet (1.5 meter) wide; the courtyard smaller; the rooms like pearls strung on a thread. Pre-existing mango trees are woven into the overall layout, referencing its grove-like plot while providing respite from, and directionality for, the breezes flowing in from beyond. Jaalis and verandah floors are finished in terracotta brick, providing both visual and tactile cooling.

23.
BINH HOUSE
VTN
ARCHITECTS

HO CHI MINH CITY, VIETNAM

House area:
233 m²

Plot area:
321 m²

Architect in Charge:
Vo Trong Nghia

Project Team:
Masaaki Iwamoto, Chiang Hsing-O, Nguyen Tat Dat,
Nguyen Duy Phuoc, Takahito Yamada

Interior Designer:
VTN Architects

Landscape Designer:
VTN Architects

Photographer:
Hiroyuki Oki, Quang Dam

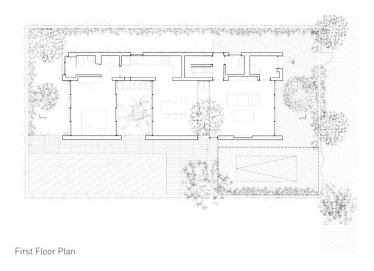

First Floor Plan

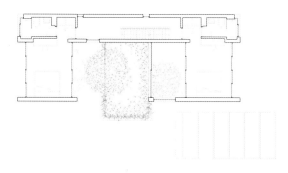

Second Floor Plan

Due to rapid urbanization, cities in Vietnam have been diverging from their origins as low density tropical green spaces. Newly developed urban areas are losing their connection with nature. Vo Trong Nghia is a local Vietnamese firm that has made it a priority to engage with natural and environmental factors wherever possible, and Binh House is but one project in the House for Trees series, prototypical housing designs which intend to provide green spaces within high density neighbourhoods.

Gardens are located on top of the various vertically stacking spaces; bound by sliding glass doors. This strategy not only improves the microclimate by using natural ventilation and daylight in every room, but the alternately stacking openings also increase visibility and interaction between residents.

Living, dining, study and bedrooms are continuously opened, while service areas such as the kitchen, bathrooms, stairs and corridors are located in the west to limit heat radiation exposure towards frequently occupied areas. The vertical variation of

spaces creates a lopsided pressure difference. Thus, when the surrounding houses are built, natural ventilation is maintained. Thanks to these passive strategies, the house always stays cool in the tropical climate. Air conditioning system is rarely used.

The roof gardens host large trees for shading, therefore reducing indoor temperature. Vegetables can also be planted to serve its resident's daily needs. This vertical farming solution is suitable for high-density housing whilst also contributing to Vietnamese way of life.

Sustainable materials such as natural stone, wood, and exposed concrete, complement the microclimate, to the point of writing the residents have never used the furnished AC. The architecture is not only to meet the functional and aesthetic concerns, but also as a means to connect people to people, and people to nature.

24.
THE GUILD
RAW
ARCHITECTURE

WEST JAKARTA, INDONESIA

House Area:
250 m²

Plot Area:
500 m²

Architect in Charge:
Realrich Sjarief

Project Team:
Septrio Effendi, Miftahuddin Nurdayat, Rio Triwardana, Tatyana
Kusumo, Jovita Lisyani Halim, Tirta Budiman, Rifandi S. Nugroho,
Hendrick Tanuwidjaja, Bambang Priyono, Hawandi Wijaya

Interior Designer:
Realrich Sjarief

Landscape Designer:
Realrich Sjarief

Photographer:
Eric Dinardi

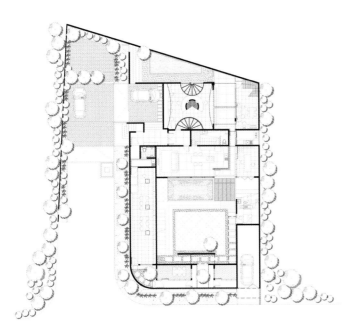

Ground Floor Plan

Conceptualized as a sanctuary, deep within the confines of Jakarta's hyper-urban chaos, The Guild hides behind an exaggerated-height border wall; a solid fence bereft of viewing access from the outside. This typology appears immutable from the outside, yet once beyond her borders, The Guild's "introverted" personality opens and blooms.

The building consists of a master bedroom, living room, studio, office, library, an open courtyard, and a kitchen. The entrance is ensconced in concrete, steel, glass, and polycarbonate sheeting. Access to the House and the Studio are separated by a 6.5 by 6.5 foot (2 by 2 meter) foyer.

The bedroom is located on the 1st floor, while the remaining spaces are located on the ground floor. The circulation is interlocked, to provide easy access to the studio below.

Hot west–to–east tropical sunlight is blocked by way of solid interspersing walls, while the façade is open to the north-south orientation. Several pyramid-shaped cutouts allow sunlight to come through the middle of the building, and allow fresh air circulation through the small gaps in between glass and concrete.

The studio consists of 19.5 by 19.5 foot (6 by 6 meter) square shape; essentially a small void with a tapered skylight made of concrete with several small gaps to provide light and air circulation. The library, which is open to the public at the weekend, is sunken at the perimeter, given the need for public access and the requirements of keeping books safe from the sun and constant temperature. At the heart of the house is a courtyard, replete with fish pond, which is backed by a 11.5 foot (3.5 meter) radius circular window which looks into the family room.

The Guild is an example of a project which utilizes modification of form and programme to not only protect from the local climate, but to take advantage of it, which is a central theme of tropical modernism in toto.

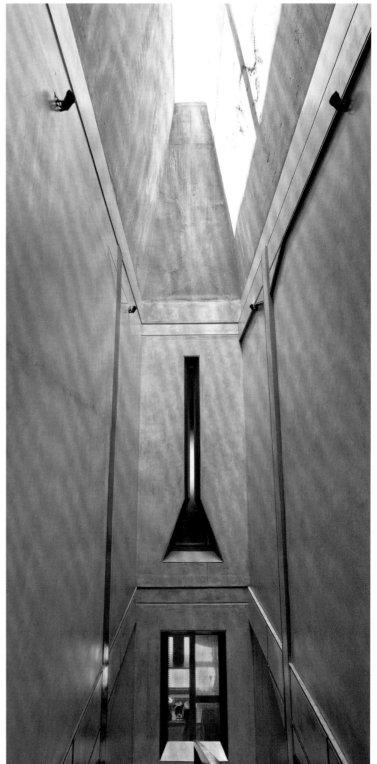

25.
BEN
HOUSE GP
WAHANA
ARCHITECTS

SOUTH JAKARTA, INDONESIA

House area:
400 m²

Plot area:
800 m²

Architect in Charge:
GeTs Architects & Wahana Architects

Project Team:
Gerard Tambunan & Rudy Kelana

Interior Designer:
Agus Gunawan

Landscape Designer:
Indogreen

Photographer:
Fernando Gomulya

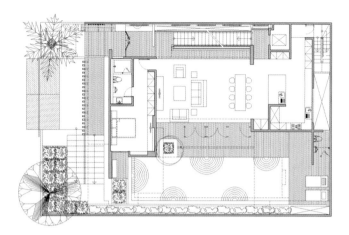

Ground Floor Plan

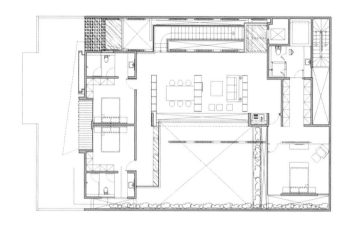

Upper Floor Plan

A bold statement about locality, materiality, and volume, Wahana Architects' Ben House GP is by turns hyper-polished and roughly locavorious. Comprised of myriad volumetric realities and theoretically oppositional material palettes, yet remaining true to the environmental, environmental, and natural principles at the heart of tropical modernism.

Located in South Jakarta, Ben House is a three-story, 800-square-meter house situated on a 400-square-meter site, where each story speaks to diverse levels of protection; the first storey as the administration zone, with the following two storeys as the semi-private and private zones.

The spatial prerequisites inspired Wahana to a complicated spatial and arrangement-oriented investigation. Unfettered passageways and floating stairs provide a pervasive sense of possibility, creating an open-concept mise-en-scène for the living and eating spaces on one side, while natural light and ventilation comes across the exterior patio and swimming pool from the other side.

On the third floor, every one of the bedrooms are joined with the family room and study; creating an interesting interspersement of germanely public and private spaces, and inspired an instinctive feeling of continuity and community. This combines with a massive vertical patio nursery—a fragile component that succeeds in obscuring that beyond the site, while adding a tropical equalization into the mix.

Focused on this nationality of three-zones, readily available local stones (including andesite and marble) overwhelm the first floor, bringing an encased air; while the second floor boasts vertical aluminium cross sections with a hint of glass adding a translucent element to the enormous façade.

Inverse clarity and softness are articulated via the wooden glass box and a skinning metal sheet, which further demonstrates the house's mixed temperament.

26.
TROPICAL
BOX HOUSE
WHBC
ARCHITECTS

KUALA LUMPUR, MALAYSIA

House area:
670 m²

Plot area:
10,500 m²

Architect in Charge:
WHBC Architects

Project Team:
Projurutek Sdn Bhd,CHB Construction,
Ming Seng Construction,Loke Electrical

Interior Designer:
Teng Designs

Landscape Designer:
WHBC Architects

Photographer:
Kent Soh

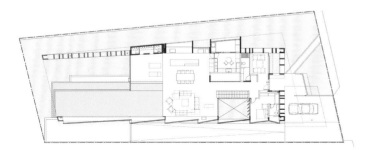

Ground Floor Plan

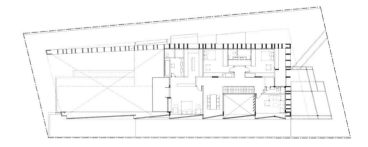

First Floor Plan

WHBC Architects' Tropical Box House combines various articulations of tropical modernism through homage to a variety of typologies, from Bawa to Gene Leedy to the Palm Springs mid-centuryists, manifesting as a concrete tropical box that embraces the lush jungle.

The project was envisioned as an inward looking abode that safeguards its interior from the tropical sun and rain while, at the same time, embraces the dense natural floral enclave that the house sits within.

Resembling a concrete egg-crate, the external frame envelopes the house to keep the heat out, while drawing daylight in, in order to create comfortable spaces within. The perforated nature of this envelope allows the existing overgrowth to grow directly into the volume of the house; softening the boundaries of inside and outside. The whole of the exterior resembles a repeating-pattern geometric brise-soleil, facilitating regulation of interior light intensity.

From the entry level, the site slopes downwards toward the rear elevation. The house's design takes advantage of the sloping terrain to keep the dampness and humidity out. Spaces are arranged to keep the majority of the house raised off the ground; nestling it amongst a canopy of trees.

The main spaces—living, dining and swimming pool—are positioned at the entry level; bedrooms are placed on the upper floor; while garage and service area sits on the lower ground. Approach to the house is via a bridge flanked by multiple mature Albizia trees. From the entrance, a relatively narrow walkway, adjacent to a stairway and an internal courtyard, leads to the open living area.

The pool and adjoining garden are enclosed within the volume of this egg-crate structure. These spaces are completely surrounded by green foliage as they hover close to the tropical canopy, creating a wholly tropical respite.

27.
BRG HOUSE
TAN TIK LAM
ARCHITECTS

BANDUNG, INDONESIA

House area:
750 m²

Plot area:
2,500 m²

Architect in Charge:
Tan Tik Lam

Project Team:
Romi Aprianda, Priesto Naray, Ade Sumi Santoso, Maman Lesmana

Interior Designer:
Tan Tik Lam Architects

Landscape Designer:
June Lie Landscape

Photographer:
Mario Wibowo

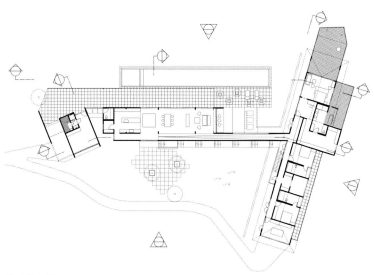

First Floor Plan

This residence designed for a young couple was conceptually influenced by the context of the site, including a stunning view of a tropical forest on the east side.

Having a huge existing site area, single story buildings were proposed for most of the functions, with a semi-basement level in some parts of the buildings for service functions.

The site is divided into two zones: a drop off area, and the main house area. An outdoor passage provides connection between the two areas, while a long and wide verandah provides entry to the main house.

A building mass with north-south axis accommodates the living area, while another one with east-west axis accommodates the more private functions of the house.

The bedrooms face the east, providing it with a stunning outdoor view, while the corridor faces the west. The two are connected by a narrow long ramp passage, creating a dramatic transition between the living area & the more private spaces. Service functions were put below the bedrooms, providing privacy for the bedrooms, while also utilizing the existing topography.

28.
SECRET GARDEN HOUSE WALLFLOWER ARCHITECTURE + DESIGN

SINGAPORE

House area:
1,291 m²

Plot area:
1,862 m²

Architect in Charge:
Robin Tan

Project Team:
Robin Tan, Cecil Chee, Sean Zheng, Shirley Tan & Eileen Kok

Interior Designer:
Cecil Chee, Wallflower Pte Ltd

Landscape Designer:
Nyee Phoe Flower Garden Pte Ltd

Photographer:
Marc Tey

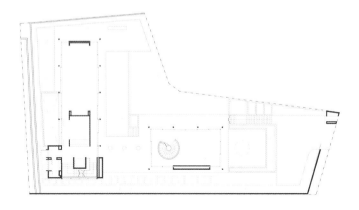

First Floor Plan

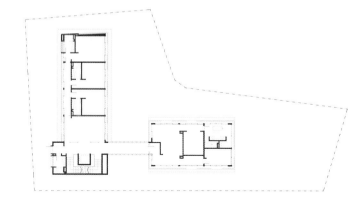

Second Floor Plan

Singapore-based Wallflower Architecture + Design conceptualized the Secret Garden House as an ode to traditional, stilted kampung houses. The entirely of the house appears to be floating a full storey off the ground, on pilotis, as much of southeast asian vernacular architecture was; surrounding a courtyard.

Visitors enter the house via a granite cave entrance leading to an "underground" lobby. A steel and glass helical floating staircase leads directly up into the heart of the communal living spaces, on the raised "ground floor," which is comprised of two rectangular travertine blocks sitting on slender pilotis. The blocks are connected at the second floor by an enclosed floating bridge. A ribbon window cuts around the travertine stone façade. Adjustable vertical timber louvers lined strategically along this band of windows shield the glazing; regulating how much sunlight reaches the interior, as well as ensuring privacy when required.

Basic tropical modern principles of orientation, thermal mass, sun-screening and natural ventilation are fundamental to the de-

sign. It is a house designed for the tropics, expressed by modern materials and contemporary aesthetics. Every floor is designed to be cross-ventilated.

Primary to the design ethos are cross-ventilating breezes.. In the basement, air flows through the large cave-like garage opening, through the timber slatted lobby and exits via a sizeable sunken garden courtyard at the rear that is open to the sky. Above ground, the lifted bedroom blocks are kept passively cool by layers of masonry, air cavities, travertine stone cladding, roof gardens and pergolas. Skylights further animate the experience in the course of the day through ever-shifting shafts of light. The entire home can, of course, be closed off to the tropical climate, but is designed specifically to take advantage of it.

29.
HOUSE 24
PARK +
ASSOCIATES

SINGAPORE

House area:
715 m²

Plot area:
995 m²

Architect in Charge:
Lim Koon Park

Project Team:
Christina Thean, Wong Zi Xin, Jeeraporn Prongsuriya,
Mutiara Herawati

Interior Designer:
Park + Associates

Landscape Designer:
Green Prospect Pte Ltd

Photographer:
Edward Hendricks

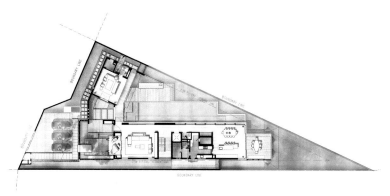

First Floor Plan

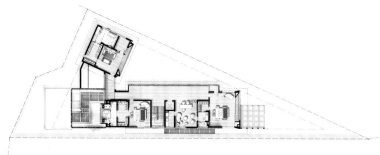

Second Floor Plan

In a usual circumstance, the front of the house is the most important—not in this case. House 24 is sited on a triangular plot, a constraint that the architects took on as an opportunity to really engage with the siting and planning of the house, in order to achieve a meaningful footprint that actualised the client's spatial, functional, and privacy requirement. Moreover, the site adjoins a lushly landscaped state land that we endeavoured to take advantage of at every available opportunity and every habitable space.

As such, the architects turned the house away from the main road and neighbouring houses, and instead have the living spaces open out to the mature greenery beyond. The result is a massing comprising of two blocks which, when combined, define a V-shaped patio on the first floor that becomes the focal point of common activities and entertainment, borrowing views from the surrounding greenery.

The courtyard screen fronting the street is an exercise in rethinking the conventional entry sequence of residential dwellings, and

an exploration in creating a more layered and sequential experience. It is experienced almost as a ritual space—serene and tranquil—marking the transition between the public and private.

It was also an opportunity to explore what timber craftsmanship might mean in contemporary architecture, and we envisioned the screen to be a well-crafted element with modern aesthetic and detailing. It eventually manifested itself as a refined and rhythmic facade, drawing attention to its delicate scale even as a structure that is over 26 feet (8 meters) high. A delightful pattern of light and shadow plays out over the course of each day whilst allowing sunlight to filter in and natural air to stream in, creating a relaxing ambience that reinforces the client's desire to live in a home that reflected its tropical locality.

30.
RIDOUT
ROAD HOUSE
BEDMaR & SHi

SINGAPORE

House area:
1,490 m²

Plot area:
2,590 m²

Architect in Charge:
Ernesto Bedmar

Project Team:
Ernesto Bedmar and Juliana Chan

Landscape Designer:
Ernesto Bedmar

Photographer:
Claudio Manzoni and Albert Lim

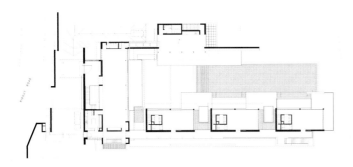

First Floor Plan

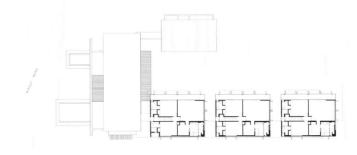

Second Floor Plan

The Ridout Road House is amongst BEDMaR & SHi's most important, and highly respected, projects. Tasked with creating a single property to house the owners and their two adult children, Bedmar was essentially asked to create three independent dwellings within the broader framework of a shared house.

The house is entered from the west side, past an intentionally rough hewn, multi-coloured stone wall, instantly creating a stark juxtaposition with the understated sophistication of a positively enormous blonde wood front door. A subtle foyer opens directly into the main shared living area; a single-storey transitional collective space that encompasses living room, dining room, and library/family room spaces, demarcated only by negative space and furniture layout.

The property's layout focuses on an internal courtyard of manicured gardens and a lengthy swimming pool tiled in muted aquamarine, bordered to the west by the terrace, to the north by a pool pavilion, and to the south by three patios for each of the main suites.

Each suite is two stories; the upper consisting of three bedrooms, two bathrooms, and a terrace, while the lower consists of living and dining rooms, alongside powder room and kitchen, as well as a large patio overlooking the central courtyard. Living/dining rooms in the individual suites feature sliding glass walls that are fully openable, mirroring the typology of the main common entertaining space, further eliminating the difference between indoor and outdoor spaces.

The Ridout Road House's juxtaposition of collaborative and differentiated space is perfectly demonstrative of BEDMaR & SHi's modern iteration of the Balinese compound archetype; the village as villa. This residence is a statement of purpose; Bedmar's intuitive delineation of the need for privacy in situations of proximity, and solution to the parallel needs for both private and shared spaces.

31.
CHANCERY
LANE
BEDMaR & SHi

NOVENA, SINGAPORE

House area:
1,247 m²

Plot area:
1,862 m²

Architect in Charge:
Ernesto Bedmar

Project Team:
Ernesto Bedmar and Juliana Chan

Interior Designer:
BEDMaR & SHi

Landscape Designer:
BEDMaR & SHi

Photographer:
Claudio Manzoni

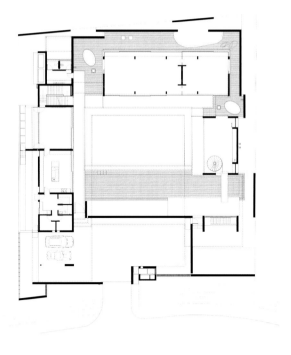

First Floor Plan

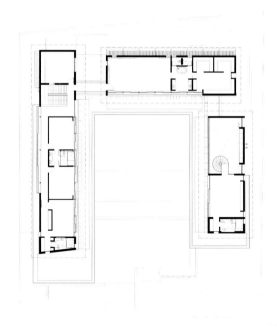

Second Floor Plan

Ernesto Bedmar has long since proved himself a modern master of the tropical modernist genre. His work throughout the region has continuously demonstrated his thoughtfulness, intuition, awareness, and ongoing determination to parse and promote the best of the genre across myriad influences and aesthetic variations.

The Chancery Lane house is an icon of contemporary tropical modernism; one that has been studied and discussed by students and professors, feted by books and magazines, and presumably lusted after by a large portion of Singapore's citizenry.

Evocative of the simple, open structures of times past, yet possessed of a modernity of spirit perfectly in keeping with contemporary life. The house conflates, rather than juxtaposes, indoor and outdoor spaces in perfect harmony.

The building itself is laid out in a U formation, with the house oriented around a central courtyard comprised of a large rectangular swimming pool floored with dramatic polished blue and

black stone, and a sheltered outdoor bbq and living space. A pair of structures made into a single one, distinguished between the west and northern cross-sections via floating bridges on the second floor.

On the side, three individual "townhouses" share a single, elongated flat roof which boasts overhanging eaves. As the client's programmatic requirements indicated full service residences for the master and mistress of the house, as well as for their two grown children (and their families), the private quarters manifest as three distinct "houses," each of which is two stories, with a spacious upstairs master suite, as well as living quarters, kitchen, pantry, and guest washroom downstairs. Slatted wooden louvers close off entirely when privacy is sought.

All spaces are naturally directed inwards, utilizing the central courtyard as a natural focal point, underscoring the dramatic symbiosis between indoor and outdoor space.

32.
CASABLANCKA
RESIDENCE
BUDIPRADONO
ARCHITECTS

BALI, INDONESIA

House Area:
573 m²

Plot Area:
808 m²

Architect in Charge:
Budi Pradono

Project Team:
Arief Mubaraq, Hendrawan Setyanegara, Eka Feri Rudianto,
Anggita yudisty Zurman Nasution

Interior Designer:
Rini Blanckaert

Landscape Designer:
Budipradono Architects

Photographer:
Fernando Gomulya

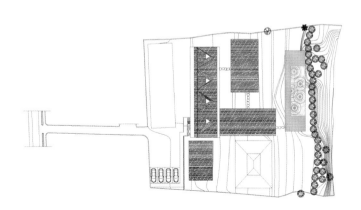

Roof Plan

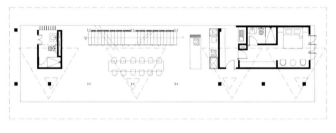

Ground Floor Plan

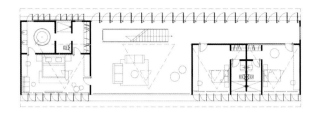

First Floor Plan

Designed as an homage-cum-reinterpretation of traditional Bali-nese architecture, the Casablancka residence develops the spa-tial concept of Tri Mandala, which describes three realms; Nista Mandala, the outer and lower mundane less-sacred realm, Madya Mandala, the intermediate middle realm, and Utama Mandala, the inner and higher most important sacred realm.

It also borrows strongly from traditional Balinese buildings known as Taring; which are temporary structures made of bamboo, typi-cally used for weddings and other celebrations. Taring have a dis-tinct separation between floors, walls, and roofs. It is this aspect that Budi-Pradano chose to focus on, in a dazzling mixture of tra-ditionalism and modernism.

The house's mandate was to interact seamlessly with nature. Walls are made of local brick (which are in-filled with concrete), and arranged in zig-zag patterns, which modulates heat trans-ference, while retaining aesthetic parity with the region's natural colour palette of soft browns and rich oranges.

The building's meant to be as open as possible, with an interior concept manifesting as a dialogue between East and West. The majority of the furniture is built of reclaimed materials circa the 1940s Indonesian Dutch period. The interpretations are made modern by way of a palette of soft blues and whites fabric. The remainder of the furnishings continue the theme by virtue of using antique Javanese accent pieces.

The exterior bamboo structure stands independently as a columned structure and supporting roof, allowing natural light to enter the build-ing through the glass partitions above the brick walls. Flooring is of lo-cal cement, and a multicoloured handmade Javanese cement which was frequently used in colonial buildings of the 1930s.

A roof of flattened bamboo, is shaped to be reminiscent of the lo-cal mountains, representing the relationship between the people and the sky.

PACIFIC

SOLIS HAMILTON ISLAND QLD | RENATO D'ETTORRE ARCHITECTS
PLANCHONELLA HOUSE | JESSE BENNETT
OCEAN HOUSE | OLSON KUNDIG

33.
SOLIS,
HAMILTON
ISLAND QLD
RENATO
D'ETTORRE
ARCHITECTS

HAMILTON ISLAND, AUSTRALIA

House area:
373 m²

Plot area:
2,335 m²

Architect in Charge:
Renato D'Ettorre

Project Team:
Thomas Wagner

Interior Designer:
Belinda Brown

Landscape Designer:
Renato D'Ettorre Architects and Hortus Design

Photographer:
Mads Mogensen

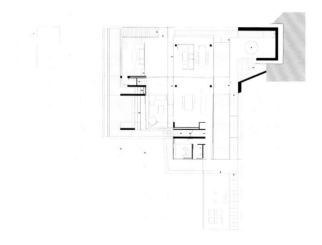

Ground Floor Plan

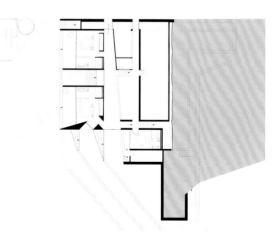

Lower Floor Plan

Solis House draws inspiration from its magnificent location and Mediterranean coastal architecture: simple, permeable volumes that open and unfold, capturing distant views of tropical waters and island life. The house offers an idyllic experience of casual, elegant outdoor living amidst the beauty and tranquility of Hamilton Island.

Built over three inter-locking levels, the design intends to highlight the relationship between interior and exterior environments, and to capture the serenity of the natural surroundings of the built form. Terraces are fluid extensions of internal spaces capturing cooling breezes and allowing cross ventilation. Bedroom terraces frame magnificent views of water and gardens. Always connected to and taking inspiration from water, the interiors are sheltered and cool, incorporating swimming pools, reflecting ponds, and strategically positioned trickling waterfalls.

White and primary colours were not permissible by local building authorities so concrete was the primary material employed for its

eternal qualities of extreme resiliency, excellent thermal properties and textural quality. Floor and wall finishes, such as polished concrete and honed travertine tiles were selected for their durability and tactile qualities.

The architecture in Solis House incorporates a number of passive climate controls, such as deep overhangs that shade the interior, massive concrete walls, green roofs, natural ventilation, use of water as cooling elements, and water collection via rainwater tanks.

The elimination of all periphery walls, except those required for privacy and structural reasons, means a spirit-lifting view is visible from all living spaces. The use of water throughout, in swimming pools, lily-strewn reflection ponds and strategically positioned waterfalls, adds to the serenity of this unique home.

34.
PLANCHONELLA
HOUSE
JESSE BENNETT

CAIRNS, AUSTRALIA

House area:
280 m²

Plot area:
4,818 m²

Architect in Charge:
Jesse Bennett

Project Team:
Jesse Bennett and Anne-Marie Campagnolo

Interior Designer:
Anne-Marie Campagnolo

Landscape Designer:
Jesse Bennett and Anne-Marie Campagnolo

Photographer:
Sean Fennessy

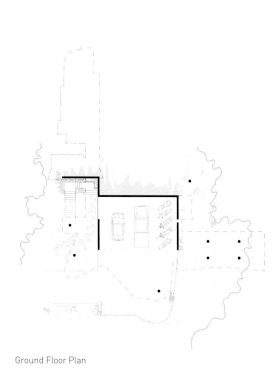

Ground Floor Plan

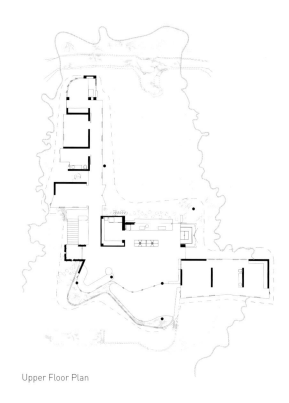

Upper Floor Plan

Planchonella House was conceptualized with a simple idea in mind—to create a series of joyful spaces to inspire and enrich daily life. Set in the verdant tropics of Australia's north Queensland, the house embraces the surrounding heritage rainforest, and utilizes experimental passive design methods. The straightforward approach and use of Lo-Fi technologies results in a raw and honest dwelling.

Contours of the site ridgeline formed the basis for the playful curvilinear lines manifested in concrete. As not to protrude out with the ridge, the profile is mirrored and cuts back in to the ridge, leaving overhangs above and below the exterior window barriers (the lower being transformed into small gardens that provide an extra sense of greenery. The wings on each side of the ridge float into the surrounding rainforest, giving the sense that the house is actually part of the tree canopy.

The large flat roof, with its undulating cantilever, acts as a rainforest canopy above, while minimal walls and columns in between allow for unobstructed views of the landscape. This omission of boundaries between inside and outside gives an openness and quality of space that borders on surreality; the sense that the occupant is living completely within the external landscape.

The plan wraps around the courtyard space, which is considered the central hearth of the dwelling. The courtyard contributes much to the house and its occupants. It is an oasis that provides sun, light, ventilation, happiness, activity, visual stimulation, and entertainment. It also provides connection to the surrounding rainforest;connection from one part of the house to another; and acts as the focal node to the promenade experience of moving through the house.

Much is made of the modernist aspects of this architectural genre. Jesse Bennett has, with this dwelling, reminded us of the cruciality of the tropical aspect.

35.
OCEAN HOUSE
OLSON KUNDIG

HAWAII, UNITED STATES

House area:
1,207 m²

Plot area:
N/A

Architect in Charge:
Jim Olson

Project Team:
Kevin M. Kudo-King

Interior Designer:
Anne Gunderson

Landscape Designer:
David Tamura

Photographer:
Paul Warchol and Jim Olson

Ground Floor Plan

In its purest form, tropical modernism is borne entirely of post-vernacular interpretations by the iconic Sri Lankan architect Geoffrey Bawa, whose work essentially birthed the genre through careful, considered, and articulate explorations of contemporary architectural advancements on the intuitive machinations of traditional tropical design.

The Ocean House, designed by Olson Kundig, and situated on Hawaii's lush and largely unspoiled Big Island, was conceptualized as a temple of isolation; a beautiful fortress whose sole protective responsibility is the occupants comfort and relaxation. A sunny sanctuary that both espouses and typifies modernist conveniences, while taking significant cues from both traditional Balinese courtyard residences and temples. Demonstrably inspired by traditional Balinese palaces and temples, the house sits on a beautiful promontory of exposed lava on the island of Hawaii. Tropical design concepts and time-honoured building practices were used to ensure that the house fir naturally into its setting.

The lava base anchors the house to the site, while the roof planes appear to float in the sky. Broad overhangs protect the interior from the sun, while sliding window "walls" open to unite the indoors and outdoors, and cool the house using natural breezes for cross-ventilation. A river of hardened lava runs through the site and symbolically connects the house to traditional Pacific island sources of energy; focussing on the mountains and the sea.

The house's setting is a paradise of greenery, punctuated by mature palm trees. High concept vernacular propositions exist in the form of treated concrete walls, a multi-pavilion footprint, low-slung, pitched roofs that provide plenty of shade and protection from the elements, glossed wood interior touches, and antique local accent pieces that tie everything together.

APPENDIX

ARCHITECTS PROFILES

 **ANG, BC AND HSIA, WEN** The partners of Malaysian firm WHBC Architects describe themsleves as "no background," "no pe-degree" "blue collar architects." BC is the epitome of the term "home grown." He finished his studies at UTM before establishing the company with his wife and business partner, Wen Hsia. They operate from their home-cum-office with their trusty sidekick and furry friend named Abu. There's something unconventional about the down-to-earth couple that reflects in the work they put out.

 **ANTONI, STEFAN** completed his bachelor of architecture degree at the University of Cape Town in 1985 with a first class pass. In 1987 he set up the architectural practice Stefan Antoni Architects, which is today known as SAOTA—Stefan Antoni Olmesdahl Truen Architects. Stefan Antoni is considered one of a number of architects who have contributed to setting a new standard of design and professionalism in the top end of the domestic market in South Africa.

 **BARROSO, HÉCTOR** decided to open his own office in 2010, with nothing but his computer, pencil, and paper. Six years later, he has five collaborators working with him. Barroso prizes the creation of rich atmospheres to make timeless projects that can grow old with dignity, which he conceptualizes through art, music, and walking the streets looking for inspiration. His goal is an honest architecture, of apparent concrete, without finishes or makeup, with clear lines of unique personality, according to its climate and orientation.

 **BEDMAR, ERNESTO** completed his Bachelors of Architecture in 1980 from the University of Architecture & Town Planning,Cordoba, Argentina. He is a Registered Architect in both Argentina and Singapore, as well a Corporate Member of the Singapore Institute of Architects. His career began in 1977 when he did practical work in the studio at Miguel Angel Roca, in Argentina. In 1980 he became an Associate at Miguel Angel Roca, South Africa, and designed a town planning project for Protea New Town—South Africa, before ultimately launching his firm in Singapore.

 **BENNETT, JESSE** established a small architecture and interior design firm, with the philosophy of creating joyful places and spaces that inspire and enrich daily life. The firm is best described as a tight-knit husband and wife team working in collaboration with a network of skilled local craftsmen and engineers. Jesse is both a registered Architect and Builder, and his background includes working at leading architectural and design firms, as well as alongside esteemed architect,Drew Heath.

BRILLHART, JACOB founded Brillhart architecture in 2005, after completing his Masters in Architecture from Columbia University. Jacob complements his practice by teaching design, freehand drawing, and architectural theory as an Assistant Professor at the University of Miami School of Architecture. A Gabriel Prize finalist in 2006 and 2007, and a finalist for the 2010 Rome Prize in Architecture, Brillhart has also served as the Favrot Visiting Assistant Professor at Tulane University.

BUCCI, ANGELO graduated from his architecture studies at the University of São Paulo in 1987, and completed his Doctorate there in 2005. He has been an Honorary Member of the American Institute of Architects (AIA) since 2011. In 2003 he founded the practice SPBR Arquitectos, after leaving the practice MMBB architects, which he co-founded and directed between 1996 and 2002. He is a Professor at the Faculty of Architecture and Urbanism of the University of São Paulo, and has served as Visiting Professor at Universities including ETH in Zurich, Yale, Buenos Aires, IUAV Venice, M.I.T., and Harvard GSD.

CAFARDO, SAMANTA graduated from FAU-Mackenzie in 1997, then did a post-grad specialization in Large Scale Projects at UPC in Barcelona. Her project 'From Local to Global' won the Europandom Award, while her Manguetown Project received the 2001 Dutch Amphibious Living Award from Kunstgebouw. In 2002 she joined her university colleagues at Studio mk27; as one of the initial group of co-authors of the firm.

CHONG ROBIN, TAN CHAI completed all his Bachelor of Architecture with Honours from the National University of Singapore in 1995. Shortly thereafter he completed the Jurong Town Corporation project while working at the prestigious firm, BEDMaR & SHi. In 1999, he established Wallflower Architecture + Design, a Singaporean firm fêted for innovative and environmentally conscious architecture.

DAOLIO, JOÃO PAULO AND DUARTE, THIAGO NATAL, founded Obra Arquitectos. João studied at FAUUSP between 1998 and 2004 and at TUDELFT in Delft, The Netherlands, in 2002. Thiago also studied at FA-UUSP between 1998 and 2004 and at TUDELFT in Delft, The Netherlands, in 2002. They are known for their intuitive modern tropical residences with nods to classical Brazilian brutalism, and a harmonious interaction between architecture and environment.

D'ETTORRE, RENATO Born in Italy, moved to Australia with his family in the 1960's, studied architecture at the University of Technology, Sydney. In 1984 Renato lived in Sardinia investigating many architectural sites around the mediterranean islands. He later worked for Pier Luigi Nervi and Paolo Portoghesi in Roma and Harry Seidler and Romaldo Giurgola in Sydney. Renato started his sole practice in 1990 after a commission for a house in South Coogee. The house, with a magnificent site by the sea, inspired Renato to take the opportunity to forge a personal path within the plurality of the modern architectural milieu.

JACOBSEN, PAULO AND JACOBSEN, BERNARDO founded Jacobsen Arquitetura. Paulo Jacobsen had previously been involved in the architecture of 800+ projects in various sectors, including high quality residential architecture. After his son Bernardo finished his studies, and stints working with international architects including Christian de Portzamparc and Shigeru Ban, the pair founded Jacobsen Arquitetura, which is currently developing roughly 60 projects with a team of 35 divided between their offices in Rio de Janeiro and São Paulo.

KELANA, RUDY Born in Medan in 1968, Rudy Kelana got his architecture degree from Tarumanagara University, Jakarta in 1992. He established his own architecture consultant, Wahana Architects, in 1996. Most of Rudy Kelana's projects are houses. Also, his work have already been published in several architectural magazines, such as SKALA+, LARAS and Griya Asri. TAMBUNAN, GERARD is the founder and principled architect in GeTs Architects, studio based in Jakarta, Indonesia. he has accomplished many residential projects that some of those consist of renovation projects, villas and etc. Before, he was a principle in Wahana Architects. Always explores his ideas totally to create qualified and innovative designs with limitedness found.

KHOSLA, SANDEEP AND ANAND, AMARESH are the leaders in Architecture and Interior Design in Bangalore, India; established by Sandeep Khosla in 1995. Khosla Associates, creates a versatile body of work ranging from architecture and interiors of residences and corporate offices to retail and hospitality spaces. They have won over 25 National and International Awards including the Inside Outside Designer of the Year Award, 2010. Their distinct style of tropical residential architecture uses local materials and concepts, but reinterprets them with a unique and contemporary design sensibility.

KOGAN, MARCIO graduated from the School of Architecture and Urbanism at the University Presbyterian Mackenzie in 1976. Early in his career, Marcio divided his time between cinema and architecture, in partnership with Isay Weinfeld, his University friend. In 1988, the duo produced a feature-film called *Fire and Passion*. In 2001, Marcio Kogan's office changed its name to Studio mk27, and has since gained greater international recognition. mk27's tropical residential projects have been featured frequently in myriad international architecture publications.

KOON PARK, LIM Is the founder and principal architect of Park + Associates, which was set up in 1999. At university, he chose architecture over law, reading his bachelor degree at the National University of Singapore and, later, master's at the University of Sheffield in the UK. He then started work as a graduate architect with Architects Group Associates (AGA), but quit after five years to join Loh in China for two years. He went back to AGA thereafter, then left to set up his own practice. Even with the increasing attention Park + Associates – and, indeed, Lim himself – is garnering, the affable Lim is adamant about not letting success get to his head.

MORELL SIXTO, ALBERTO graduated from the Technical School of Architecture of the Polytechnic University of Madrid in 1992, and became a Professor there in 2000. Since 2010, he has directed the Morell Teaching Unit of the Department of Architectural Projects there. In this collaborative unit of the University, focus is paid to both Project Teaching Workshops and Research Projects.

NGHIA, VO TRONG studied architecture at the University of Tokyo before returning to Vietnam to establish VTN Architects (Vo Trong Nghia Architects) in 2006. Through a series of award-winning projects, Nghia has developed sustainable architectural design by integrating inexpensive local materials and traditional skills with contemporary aesthetics and modern methodologies. Nghia has received numerous international prizes and honours, including World Architecture Festival Award, ARCASIA award, WAN 21 for 21 Award, and FuturArc Green leadership Award. In 2012, he was selected the Architect of the year in Vietnam.

OLSON, JIM is the founding principal of the Seattle-based firm Olson Kundig Architects. He is best known for residential design, often for art collectors, though his designs have also included museums, commercial spaces and places of worship. In 2006, William Stout Publishers released *Art + Architecture: The Ebsworth Collection and Residence*. His honors include the 2007 Seattle AIA Medal of Honor, selection as the 1999 Bruce Goff Chair of Creative Architecture at the University of Oklahoma, and his induction in 1990 as a Fellow of the American Institute of Architects. KUNDIG, TOM joined the firm in

1986, he has received some of the world's highest design honors, including a National Design Award in Architecture from the Cooper Hewitt Smithsonian Design Museum and an Academy Award in Architecture from the American Academy of Arts and Letters. In 2016, he was elected to the National Academy as an Academician in Architecture. Kundig is known for his elemental approach to design where rugged materials are left in raw or natural states to soften over time with exposure to the elements – and to human touch.

OPPENHEIM, CHAD is a Miami-based architect whose work encompasses all realms of design, including large-scale urban architecture, hotels and resorts, luxury homes, and interiors and furnishings. Founded in 1999, Oppenheim Architecture + Design has garnered global recognition for socially and environmentally conscious architecture, as well as setting trends in the sustainable and humanitarian sectors.

PANJABI, SANJEEV AND MERCHANT, SANGEETA established in 1995 a studio called SPASM Design Architects, who are both graduates of the Academy of Architecture, Mumbai, and started their studio with their first commission in East Africa in 1997. SPASM believes that design is an outcome of experience, a dialogue between each space and the other and a dance with light. Keeping each project in an individual light they believe in not over-thinking a design and representing a truthfulness to a singular core value – be it materiality, texture, massing, expanse or enclosure. Hence, each of their designs reflects different ethos and emotional experiences from makers to users.

PRADONO, BUDI is the founder and principal of Budipradono Architects, a eponymous cross-disciplinary studio. He studied at Duta Wacana Christian University as well as at Berlage Institute, Rotterdam. His works are published and exhibited worldwide, and have been recognized with numerous awards. Budipradono Architects is a studio with an interdisciplinary focus on contemporary lifestyle, hospitality, and urban design through an inclusive and rigorous methodology of research, expansive collaboration, and experimentation.

PUIGCORBÉ, JOAN is the founder of the eponymous Puigcorbé Arquitectes Associats (PAAS). He has worked on a variety of building styles, including libraries, schools, offices, collective and individual housing, urban planning, and furniture. He has won competitions across the globe, in Spain, France, Morocco, and Dubai, amongst others. His work has been published in myriad architecture magazines internationally, and he has lectured in both Spain and Costa Rica. He is also one of the founders of CostaRicaNaturalDesign, a company dedicated to the design, construction, and sale of unique houses in Costa Rica.

RIZO, ELÍAS completed his architecture studies at ITESO in 1992. As an architecture student he obtained an honourable mention in the Royal British Institute of Architects' International Student Contest 1991. In 1995 he completed his Postgraduate thesis, entitled "Chicago, Urban Translations"; in 1996 he completed his Masters thesis, entitled "La Gran Escala," later his "Els Nous Instruments of Architecture" at UPC in Barcelona, Spain. In 1996 he established his eponymous architecture studio, Elías Rizo Architects.

RANGR, JASMIT SINGH born in India, he spent the first part of his childhood on the coast of the Indian Ocean, before moving to London. He was educated at Saint Paul's School, focussing on Physics, Chemistry and Mathematics. During undergraduate studies at Yale University, he was strongly encouraged to pursue Architecture after an introductory class in the subject. He returned to the Yale Graduate School of Architecture, and received the Anne C. Garland award for design for his Master of Architecture thesis.

SJARIEF, REALRICH established RAW Architecture in 2011. In doing so, he re-established the 3 generation history of craftsmanship in his family, which has lasted the entire 60 year period since Indonesian Independence. Initially the practice had no name, but was eventually named the Realrich Architectural Workshop (RAW). The practice is well known for trustworthiness, quality, and authentic design innovation, as well as a mastery of building construction in Indonesia.

STRANG, MAX is the founding principal of [STRANG], a Florida-based architecture firm acclaimed for its site-specific and climate-driven designs. Through his work, Strang has consistently underscored the ongoing relevance and importance of regional modernism to an international audience. In 2016, he was elected to the prestigious College of Fellows of the American Institute of Architects (AIA), and in 2013 he received the Silver Medal from the Miami Chapter of the AIA, the highest honour the organization can bestow.

SPECHT, SCOTT is the founding principal at Specht Architects with over 25 years of experience designing and managing institutional, commercial, and residential projects. Before founding Specht Architects, he worked as a senior designer for Daniel Libeskind Architect, and collaborated with that office on its winning New York World Trade Centre master planning proposal. He also worked for several years with Kohn Pedersen Fox and Associates in New York, and was the lead designer of a number of major building projects around the world, including the Chifley Square project in Sydney, Australia. HARPMAN, LOUISE is the founder and principal of Louise Harpman PROJECTS whose work focuses on architectural design, design research, and urban design. Before founding PROJECTS, Louise Harpman was, for 20 years, a principal in the architecture and design firm Specht Harpman. She has always maintained a commitment to teaching as well as practice. She is a tenured Associate Professor at NYU's Gallatin School of Individualized Study, and an associated faculty member at the Robert F. Wagner Graduate School of Public Service and the Department of Environmental Studies. She is also a member of the Faculty Advisory Committee at the Marron Institute of Urban Management at NYU.

TIK LAM, TAN is Indonesian architect who based in Bandung, Indonesia. He has been a member of Indonesian Architect Association(IAI) since 1995 and earned several awards in local and international audience and was a nominator for the Aga Khan Award for Architecture. He has served on juries for architectural awards at the national scale, particularly in Residential category. He extends his practice to larger scale projects, commercial and public institutions.

YURI, VITAL considered one of the 25 most promising architects in Brazil, Vital has acquired a vast collection of awards, including the New York New Practices Prize (USA), the Ibero-American Biennial of Architecture (USA), The Best of Architecture (Editora Abril), The Young Architects Award and the IAB Grand Prize. After graduating in architecture from FAU-Mackenzie in 2004, he received 1st place in the Grand Prize IAB-SP 2008 Award, before winning the Young Architects Award 2009. After working with architects Carlos Bratke and Aflalo & Gasperini, Vital opened his own office in 2007.